self leadership

and the

ne
minute
manager

self leadership

and the

:01 One minute manager

increasing effectiveness through
situational self leadership

KEN BLANCHARD
SUSAN FOWLER
LAURENCE HAWKINS

HarperCollins*Publishers*

HarperCollins*Publishers*
77–85 Fulham Palace Road,
Hammersmith, London W6 8JB

www.harpercollins.co.uk

This paperback edition 2006
7

First published in the UK by
HarperCollins*Publishers* 2005

Grateful acknowledgment is made to Bristol Park Books for
permission to reprint "The Business Card Trick" from *The
Mammoth Book of Fun and Games* by Richard B. Manchester.
Copyright © 1976 by Hart Publishing Company, Inc.

ISBN-10 0-00-720810-3
ISBN-13 978-0-00-720810-4

Printed and bound in Great Britain by
Clays Ltd, St Ives plc

 *Contents*

 *Introduction*

In the last decade or so, the old deal in business has changed. In the past, the workforce traded loyalty for job security. If you showed up to work, made a good effort, and stayed out of trouble, you were usually secure in your job. When I graduated from college in the early 1960s, one of my friends got a job with AT&T and called home. His mother cried with joy. "You're set for life," she said.

Are you set for life today with any organization? No! Lifetime employment is a thing of the past. Over the last number of years, I've been trying to find out what the new deal is. Talking to top managers around the world, I've asked, "If it's not loyalty you want from your workforce today, what do you want?" The answers have been pretty universal: "I want people who are problem solvers and are willing to take initiative. I want people working for me who act like they own the place."

In other words, top managers, given a choice, would like empowered people—individuals they can respect and trust to make good business decisions, whether top managers are around or not.

Does the workforce object to that? No! In fact, I've asked people, "What do you want from an organization if job security is no longer available?" Again, the answers have been pretty universal. People today want two things. First, they want honesty. "Don't lie to us. Don't tell us at one point there will be no layoffs and then turn around a few months later and lead a major downsizing."

Second, people want opportunities to constantly learn new skills. "At some point, if I have to look for a new job—either inside or outside my present organization—I want to have better skills and be more valuable than I was before." What better way to become more valuable than to be able to take initiative, become a problem solver, and act and think like an owner.

Bingo! We have agreement. Then what's the problem? Most people will argue that most managers are not willing to let go, that they still want to maintain control. These managers talk a good game but they still want to be in charge and prefer good subordinates who follow the lead of their superiors. Today's reality in the world of work suggests that managers today, if they are to be effective, must think and act in different ways. In the 1980s, a manager typically supervised five people—the span of control was one manager to five direct reports. To be competitive, organizations today must be customer driven, cost effective, fast, flexible, and continuously improving. This has led to more mean-and-lean organizational structures where spans of control have increased considerably. It is not uncommon today to find one manager for twenty-five to seventy-five direct reports. Add to that the emergence of virtual organizations—where managers are being asked to supervise people they never meet face-to-face—and we have an entirely different landscape emerging in the world of work.

The traditional hierarchy of leadership has evolved into a new order: empowerment of individuals. The problem is no longer how to get managers to "let go"—they have no choice anymore. The problem is how to get people to grab hold and run with the ball that is being handed to them.

A number of people are taking to this empowered environment like ducks to water. But many more are becoming immobilized. In that state they act like victims, think empowerment is a four-letter word, and view their manager as an incompetent enemy. You hear people complaining, "My boss hasn't done this; my boss hasn't done that!" The truth is that most bosses today can no longer play the traditional role of telling people what, when, and how to do things. Managers just don't have time, and in many cases their people know more about the work than they do.

What's the solution? How can we help people move from a victim mind-set to flourishing as empowered problem solvers and decision makers?

Enter Susan Fowler and Laurie Hawkins.

When my wife, Margie, and I started our company in 1979 (we now have a U.S. workforce of more than 250 people and affiliates in more than thirty nations), our first consulting partner was Laurie Hawkins. We had worked with him at the University of Massachusetts, Amherst, in the early 1970s, when I was a full-time professor and Margie was finishing her doctorate. When we decided to become entrepreneurs, Laurie was ready, willing, and able to throw his hat into the ring. Over the years, Laurie has become one of our best teachers, coaches, and consultants of our core technology: Situational Leadership® II.

Recognizing that there is no best leadership style—it all depends on the situation—we have been teaching managers all over the world to be situational leaders in working one-on-one with their people as well as in leading people in teams.

Susan Fowler was already an accomplished trainer when she attended a Situational Leadership II seminar being taught by Laurie Hawkins. She grew excited about how situational leadership can not only be applied to the one-on-one and team contexts, but also to self leadership. She felt that this framework held the answer to helping people take the lead when they didn't have the power—when someone else was their manager. Susan got Laurie excited about Situational

Self Leadership and he, in turn, introduced me to Susan. The rest is history. With Susan's lead, Situational Self Leadership has become one of our three core leadership technologies and an invaluable aid to helping people find the *power* in em*power*ment.

With *Self Leadership and the One Minute Manager,* HarperCollins has completed publication of our leadership trilogy, which started with *Leadership and the One Minute Manager* and *The One Minute Builds High Performing Teams.*

The parable you are about to read tells the story of a rising ad executive by the name of Steve, who becomes immobilized by his new responsibilities. Sitting in a café writing his resignation letter, Steve meets Cayla, the essence of Situational Self Leadership. Using magic to underscore her points, Cayla teaches Steve the three tricks of self leadership.

Enjoy the story. I think you'll root for Steve as he makes the journey to self-mastery. More important, learn the three tricks of self leadership, because they will help you and everyone you work with. Take charge of your life at work, at home, and in your community.

My biggest fear is that you will read the story and think the revelations apply to someone else. Sure, it's Steve's story. But isn't it yours, too?

—Ken Blanchard

self leadership
and the
One
minute
manager

1

Do You Believe in Magic?

"Before I present you with the television commercials, print ads, and radio scripts that we have prepared for you, let me explain the underlying thinking that went into your advertising campaign."

After months of work, this was the moment Steve had been working so hard for—his first campaign proposal. And he was scared to death.

Steve distributed the spiral-bound proposal to the eleven vice presidents, and then handed one to Roger, the President of United Bank. The ten men and two women sitting in the semicircle in front of him were his clients, and they would decide if his advertising campaign was acceptable for the upcoming year.

Steve directed them to the budget section of the proposal, forwarding his PowerPoint slides to support his presentation. He detailed the percentages of the budget allocated to the creative design, production expenses, and media buys. He outlined the media recommendations and the rationale behind each one.

No one asked any questions, and Steve sensed they were just waiting to see the creative approach. The energy in the room seemed to shift as he pulled several large foam-core posters from his oversized presentation case and declared, "Since there seem to be no questions regarding the budget, let me move on to the creative approach we're recommending for television, print, radio, and direct mail."

Steve held up the storyboards depicting important frames from the television commercials and the hand-sketched layouts for the print ads. He projected the accompanying scripts and ad copy onto the screen.

After reading the radio scripts aloud, Steve sat down, took a deep breath, and waited to hear what they thought. There was an awkward pause until one of the VPs said, "You took a much lighter approach than I thought you would, but maybe that's good—it projects a friendly bank."

Another VP spoke up. "You've obviously put a lot of time and effort into this campaign."

After another awkward silence, all heads turned to the center of the semicircle as Roger announced, "This is garbage."

Everyone was stunned. No one looked at Steve, who went blank. He didn't know how to respond. He nodded his head up and down as though he were trying to shake out a thought. Realizing he had to say something, he mindlessly began gathering the boards.

"I guess we've missed the mark," he said. "I'll go back and talk to the creative team. I'll be back in touch next week."

Steve didn't remember how he got to his car. He found himself driving—but not back to the agency. There was no way he could face his creative team. Thank heaven his boss, Rhonda, was out of town. He needed to find a place where he could be alone and think. He also needed a good cup of coffee. Driving through an unfamiliar neighborhood, he happened upon a place called Cayla's Café. He went in, hoping to find relief.

He gazed around the bookstore café with its solid wood tables and matching heavy wood chairs. It was a very different place from the high-tech chrome and high energy of the ad agency. He found solace in the cave-like coolness, and at the same time was warmed by the smell of coffee mingled with newsprint. He liked being surrounded by shelves piled high with books and magazines, and hoped they could ease the dilemma nagging at him. He knew he had to face the facts. What had gone wrong? How did things get so far off track?

Steve ordered a café mocha and let the warmth of the mug seep into his palms before taking the first sip. After this latest fiasco, he was sure to be fired. Frankly, as he thought about it, he was surprised he had gotten this far.

Three years ago Steve felt as though he'd won the lottery. Rhonda, cofounder of the Creative Advertising Agency, had hired him straight out of college with a degree in marketing. He'd taken an entry-level position and quickly worked his way to lead production manager in charge of several large accounts. Last year he'd served as coproducer of the industry's awards program for outstanding ad campaigns.

Four months ago, Steve felt flattered when Rhonda gave him the opportunity to bypass the typical career path as a junior account exec on a larger account and take the account exec role on a small but well-regarded account—United Bank. Rhonda told Steve that she wanted to empower him, and that this was the perfect time to do so.

Steve saw his promotion as his chance to prove himself. If he could make a mark with United Bank, he could soon take on the more prestigious, big-budget accounts.

Or so he had thought. Now his confidence was shattered and his future in question. The meeting had unnerved him. The more he thought about the bank president's reaction, the angrier he got.

In a blinding flash of the obvious, Steve realized the real source of his failure—it was Rhonda. She'd abandoned him. Where was she when he needed her—when everything was falling apart? Why hadn't she warned him that the client was a nightmare, that the copywriter on his team was a whiner, and that the art director was an egomaniac? Rhonda was the one person who could have saved him from this humiliation, but instead, she'd "empowered" him. He had trusted her and she'd fed him to the wolves.

Now that he had proved to be a failure, Steve was sure Rhonda would fire him. He decided to beat her to the punch. She wouldn't fire him—he'd quit! He pulled out a yellow legal pad and pen to begin drafting his resignation letter.

He was just writing the first sentence when his attention was drawn to a group of young children trying to muffle their laughter as they gathered under a rustic sign claiming the area as Cayla's Magic Corner. He watched as a small, intense, black woman moved in front of the children and sat down on a simple wooden stool facing them. She rested her forearms on her thighs and leaned close to them. Not saying a word, she slowly gazed at each child with direct eye contact. Steve could have heard a pin drop.

"I am Cayla," she said softly and very slowly, enunciating each word as though revealing a great mystery. "And I am a magician."

She told them about an old Indian mystic who taught her the art of mind over matter. To demonstrate, she pulled out two rubber bands, entwined them together, and pulled and tugged to show that they could not be easily separated.

Milking the tale for all it was worth, Cayla claimed she could separate the two bands using only the power of her mind—and then she did so. The children roared their approval. It was truly magical.

Steve regained his focus and went back to writing his resignation letter, losing track of time.

"Did you enjoy the magic?"

The voice jolted him out of his deep concentration. Steve looked up and saw Cayla standing beside him. He rose awkwardly and held out his hand.

"Sorry, I hope you didn't mind—it was fun to watch you. You're a good magician. My name is Steve."

"Mind? Not at all," the woman said as she returned the handshake. "I was hoping you'd join in. My name is Cayla."

"That's your real name?"

Cayla smiled. "Yes, it really is. My parents loved the name because it means 'empowered' in Hebrew. Maybe that's where I get my magical powers," she said with a laugh.

Steve gave her a wistful smile. "I remember when I believed in magic. I also remember how disappointed I was when I realized there was no such thing as magic. But don't get me wrong—I still appreciate the skill behind the tricks."

"You don't believe in magic," she said with a sigh. "Too bad, because it looks as though you could use some."

Steve was too startled to reply. He'd had no idea he was that transparent. Cayla pulled a chair over from the adjacent table and sat down, motioning for Steve to sit as well.

"Listen," she said, gazing at Steve with the same intense eye contact she'd given the children earlier. "You are obviously a businessman, yet here you are in this bookstore at midday. You've barely touched your coffee and scone. Something is bothering you."

Encouraged by her compassionate smile, Steve told Cayla his sad story, beginning with his excitement and pride at being given his own client after less than three years with the company.

"But it wasn't long before my dream turned into a nightmare," he explained. "Even in the initial client meetings we struggled to establish an advertising budget. I had developed media and production budgets in the past, but I couldn't tell the client what was appropriate for them. Nothing in those early meetings confirmed their good first impression of me or the agency—and it went downhill from there.

"There was no budget, no goals, and no strategy. I didn't know how to direct my creative team without an agreed-upon advertising strategy. The client drove me crazy—no one could agree on anything!"

Cayla nodded thoughtfully as she listened to Steve pour out his side of the failed client relationship. "What about your creative team? Did they help?" she asked.

"Oh, they're another story. Creative people are worse than spoiled children. I tried to give them direction, but it was like herding cats. When they asked for more specifics, I tried to explain that the client couldn't agree on a strategy. But it all fell on deaf ears. They just told me that it was my job to figure out what the client wants, even if the client isn't sure! How am I supposed to do that? Finally, I demanded they come up with something—anything—that I could show the client. So they did."

"I'm afraid to ask . . ." Cayla's statement trailed into silence.

"That's why I'm here. It was a fiasco. The client hated it. Heck, I hated it. I knew it was no good, but it was all I had." Steve was holding his head in his hands as though the burden was too much to contemplate. "I'm sick to death of the whole creative process. I'm not creative, so I have to depend on my team, and they're totally undependable! It puts me in a no-win situation. How am I supposed to manage the creative process when I'm not creative?"

Cayla pressed on. "So what do you do now?"

"I'm writing my resignation letter," Steve said matter-of-factly.

"Hmm," Cayla said thoughtfully. "Quitting?"

"Yeah, before I get fired," Steve responded.

"Why don't you go to your boss for help?" Cayla asked.

"It's too late. What can Rhonda do now? We're probably going to lose the client—and she'll blame me, even though it's not my fault."

"Whose fault is it?" Cayla asked.

Steve shook his head, feeling even more betrayed by Rhonda. "Isn't it obvious? When Rhonda abandoned me, it all fell apart. Now I've even lost confidence in the things I used to do well, like budgets, media, and production. I didn't realize advertising is such a dog-eat-dog world. It's not like I thought it would be," Steve lamented.

"Just like the magic," Cayla interjected. "You loved magic when you were naïve and could suspend your disbelief. But now you are disillusioned by it, because you realize there's a trick behind the magic."

"I'm not sure there's any trick behind succeeding in this business. If there is, no one has bothered to show me," Steve said defiantly.

"If you don't mind me saying so, it sounds as though you're full of excuses—a poor victim of circumstance."

Cayla's comment struck Steve as harsh and he replied defensively. "What do you mean, 'a victim of circumstance'?"

"I mean a person who refuses to take responsibility for the situation he's in. It's easier to blame everyone else around you, rather than taking responsibility for yourself," Cayla replied without apology.

"Hold on. You can't blame me for what's happened. Rhonda's expectations were unfair. I didn't get the support I needed from her or from the creative team— I could go on and on," Steve asserted.

"So," continued Cayla, "Rhonda should have known better than to delegate the account to you and give you the freedom to do your job, right?"

Steve was a little annoyed—and surprised—at the turn the conversation had taken. Yet in his heart he knew there was some truth to what she was saying.

Cayla's eyes filled with empathy and in a soothing voice she said, "Right now you're feeling confused and unsure. You sense there's some truth in what I'm saying, but buying into it would mean that *you* must be the responsible one—not Rhonda, your client, or your temperamental creative team. Somehow that doesn't feel fair. You're even feeling a little scared."

Steve stared at Cayla, wondering how this woman could know all that. It was as though she could read his mind.

"Let me explain," Cayla offered before Steve could ask. "I can't read your mind. As a magician, I'm a master of observation, although right now you're not all that hard to read."

Cayla paused thoughtfully and looked straight into his eyes. "Steve," she said, "years ago I was in a boat very similar to the one you're sinking in. Fortunately for me, I met a wonderful guy known as the One Minute Manager. What he taught me created such a miraculous change in my life that I call it magic. I'd like to pass that magic on to you."

"Magic?" Steve asked incredulously. "I think I need more than smoke and mirrors to deal with this mess!"

"It isn't in smoke and mirrors," Cayla said flatly. "The magic comes from self leadership."

Steve was quick to reply. "Leadership might work for the One Minute Manager, but I'm not a manager—let alone a famous one. I'm a lowly account executive with a manager who doesn't support me—not when it counts."

Cayla lifted an eyebrow. "That's how it looks from where you're sitting now—which is on the pity pot." She smiled as she said it, and Steve couldn't suppress a chuckle. "You have to turn the problem upside down," Cayla continued, "so that you're the one on top. It's time to stop looking for excuses and start leading yourself."

"Thanks for the pep talk, but I don't believe in pop psychology or magic bullets," Steve said glumly.

"I need you to suspend your disbelief, as you did when you were a child watching magic and believing. I need you to believe in the magic of self leadership," Cayla said.

Steve half-grinned as he asked, "All right, what's the trick?"

"Actually, there are three tricks. I'll share them with you when you are ready."

"How do I know when I'm ready?"

"You are ready for self leadership when you take responsibility for your own success."

Steve thought for a moment before responding. "You mean I have to stop blaming Rhonda, my creative team, and the client and ask myself what I did or didn't do to succeed?"

"Yes," she replied. "You need to stop thinking of 'empowerment' as a four-letter word and realize that it is a grand opportunity. You need to start taking the lead to get what you need."

There was a long pause as Steve pondered Cayla's challenge. Finally, he said in a soft voice, "I think I understand. Rhonda empowered me to do a job, and I failed to take the initiative and responsibility for succeeding in it. I played the role of a victim. The problem with being empowered is that when things go wrong, you have no excuses. There's no one to blame but yourself."

"Here's the truth of it: There's only power in empowerment if you are a self leader." Cayla waited for Steve's eye contact. "Remember:

*

Empowerment Is Something
Someone Gives You.
Self Leadership
Is What You Do
To Make It Work.

*

"I obviously failed the self leadership test. But I can't afford for my resume to reflect that I was fired— even if I deserve it. I've got my resignation letter almost finished," Steve declared.

"Whoa!" Cayla held up her hand. "There you go again with the pity party! What happened to self leadership?"

"That's what I'm doing," Steve argued. "I'm taking the initiative and quitting!"

Cayla shook her head and laughed. "There are times when quitting is appropriate, but this isn't one of them. Why are you so convinced that you don't have a chance? No one has actually warned you, have they?"

"No, but I know what Rhonda will think," Steve said defiantly.

"Steve, is this statement true or false? 'People are not mind readers, so it is unfair to expect them to know what you are thinking.' "

"True, with you being the possible exception," Steve said with a smile.

Cayla smiled back. "So if Rhonda can't possibly know what you are thinking, how are you so sure you know what she is thinking?"

Steve knew she had nailed him. "You have a point," he said.

"What about this statement? 'It is in my own best interest to take responsibility for getting what I need to succeed in my job.' "

"I guess the responsibility is mine," Steve agreed hesitantly, "but I'm not sure what to do."

"Follow me," Cayla said.

2

People Are Not Mind Readers

Steve followed Cayla to the back of the store and saw her slip through a door with a small nameplate bearing her name. When he reached the doorway of Cayla's office, he stood transfixed. Inside was a forest of shelves, boxes, barrels, trunks, and cabinets stuffed with magic paraphernalia. It was an enchanted place, not because of the things in it, but because of the feeling he got when he entered the room.

Cayla went over to an old oak filing cabinet labeled "Magic of Self Leadership." She opened the top drawer, riffled through files, and pulled out a sheet as she exclaimed, "Abracadabra!"

Steve laughed despite himself, caught up in Cayla's joy at finding a single piece of paper.

"Your homework for this afternoon," she said, handing him the sheet.

Instructions: Rank the following workplace motivators according to their importance to you. Place the ranking (one through ten) beside the motivator, with one being most important and ten being the least.

___ Interesting work

___ Full appreciation of work done

___ Feeling of being "in" on things

___ Job security

___ Good wages

___ Promotion and growth within the organization

___ Good working conditions

___ Personal loyalty to employees

___ Sympathetic help with personal problems

___ Tactful disciplining

"Rank the motivators on this sheet in order of their importance to you, one through ten—with one being the most important and ten being the least important. *Then,*" Cayla emphasized, "you are to ask at least five of your colleagues at work for their rankings. Bring it all back to me tomorrow and tell me what you learned."

"Is this a trick?" Steve asked skeptically.

"It's the beginning of one!" Cayla said enthusiastically. "What you learn from this assignment will reinforce what you learned today and lead you to the first trick of being a self leader."

"Okay, I'll go along with this for now—but I'm not saying I won't quit. I have until my boss gets back at the end of the month to make up my mind." Saying the words filled Steve with foreboding. He had never left a job under negative circumstances. "If you don't mind me asking, what's in this for you?"

Cayla smiled. "Remember the One Minute Manager guy I told you about? After he got me out of my mess, I asked him how I could repay him for all his insight and help. He told me that the one thing I could do was to pass on the learning to others.

"Besides," she continued with a wink, "my life vision is to be a magician. You are giving me an opportunity to do magic." Cayla's warmth and sincerity left Steve feeling comfortable about moving ahead.

"I guess I *could* use a little magic right now," he admitted: "I'll see you tomorrow."

* * *

Steve arrived back at the agency and virtually hid when one of his team members happened by. He knew he'd have to face them tomorrow at the scheduled meeting, but he wasn't ready to face his failure just yet.

As inconspicuously as possible, he made photocopies of the sheet Cayla had given him and considered which colleagues to survey. He decided to start with someone who would cooperate without needing a mountain of explanation: Rhonda's assistant, Phyllis.

He dropped the survey in Phyllis's office and followed up by sending a voicemail alerting her to check her inbox. He then took a couple of minutes to rank his own sheet.

Just before the end of the day, Steve journeyed to Phyllis's office to pick up her sheet.

"Oh, Steve, I finished your survey. It's very interesting. You'll let me know what you learn when your study is complete?" As usual, Phyllis greeted Steve with warmth and a professionalism developed over many years as an executive assistant. Phyllis could probably run the agency, but she seemed very content with her role as behind-the-scenes support.

Before Steve could respond, Grant popped his head in. "What survey?" he asked.

Steve couldn't believe Grant's boldness. Other people seemed to find the up-and-coming junior account executive quite charming, but Steve thought he was frivolous and shallow. Despite his reservations, Steve handed Grant a photocopied sheet. After all, he needed four more people to complete the survey.

Before Steve knew it, he had handed the survey out to Mike from the mailroom, Skye from information services, and a couple of others he didn't even know very well.

When Grant gave his survey back to Steve, he said with a warm smile, "No offense, Steve, but I don't see how this list is going to prove anything. I mean, it's pretty obvious that interesting work is what really motivates people."

When others heard this, it started a raging debate over the most important motivators. As the noise level escalated, Ricardo, one of the agency's senior partners, came out of his office to investigate. The Madison Avenue–dressed exec took a look at the list and said, "Well, it seems obvious to me."

Steve's heart sank, because he assumed that Ricardo would validate Grant's opinion.

"All of you have asked for more money in the past, so I guess that's what motivates you!" Ricardo said.

The group stood in quiet surprise. None of them had mentioned good wages in their top three choices. Grant had argued for interesting work; Phyllis felt that appreciation was more important; Skye had listed good working conditions. Each one of them had their own rationale for their ranking.

As people shared their answers with Ricardo, Steve observed the exec's discomfort. Ricardo looked embarrassed for not recognizing what motivated the people he employed, and Steve sensed that this made him suddenly feel inadequate.

Hoping to help alleviate Ricardo's feelings of self-doubt, Steve said, "That's the point of this exercise! Each of us has different things that motivate us. Grant's energy demands interesting work. Phyllis probably favors the feeling of being appreciated, because so much of her work is in support of others. In fact, what motivates you today may change tomorrow."

Steve looked at the mailroom clerk. "For example, when Mike's kids get older and he's thinking about sending them to college, good wages may go to the top of his list."

"Okay," Grant allowed, "maybe different things motivate each of us. Is that the point?"

Steve thought about his discussions with Cayla. Supposedly this survey would reinforce what he'd learned earlier and lead to the first trick of self leadership. Suddenly, the dots connected in Steve's mind.

"The point is, our bosses are not mind readers!" he exclaimed. "How in the world can we expect them to understand what motivates each of us? It's not fair to them—or to us."

Feeling true excitement about his insight, Steve looked at each of his colleagues one by one, then declared:

＊

Ultimately, It's In
Your Own Best
Interest To Accept
Responsibility
For Getting What
You Need
To Succeed In
The Workplace.

＊

Ricardo looked relieved—and impressed. "When we get a chance, let's talk more about this, Steve. Right now, I've got an early dinner meeting to get to. But it seems that there's something we could all learn from your little survey."

Grant patted Steve on the back as he turned to leave. "Good show!"

The others took their cues and went their own ways. Phyllis stared intently at Steve as he stood motionless in her doorway.

"Are you okay?" she asked. "You look confused."

Steve was slow to answer. "I *am* confused. I think the point of the survey is to demonstrate that a boss can't possibly know everything we need, so we should take responsibility for ourselves."

"Okay, that's a great lesson. So, where's the confusion?"

"I don't know. I think there's something else I need to learn, but I'm not sure what it is," Steve replied, deep in thought.

"You're a smart guy. I bet you figure it out," Phyllis said optimistically. "Let me know when you do." With that she went back to work at her computer.

Steve was not only confused, but ill at ease as well. He felt he was leaving something unsettled. He was the type who hated an unfinished crossword puzzle. He spotted typos better than most copy editors and he actually liked having rules and clearly defined steps to follow. But here he was, up in the air about so many things. He was scared of being fired but unsure about resigning; troubled by this strange magic woman named Cayla but curious why she felt more like a guardian angel than a stranger. He was also eager to be a self leader but conflicted about the responsibility it demanded.

He thought about Cayla's words: *I need you to believe in the magic of self leadership.* Did he believe in magic? It would be a restless night for Steve.

3

Elephant Thinking

The next morning Steve pulled up to Cayla's Café and parked in a spot just outside the storefront. A little chime rang as he entered the door—a melodious signal to the clerks that someone might need their help. As he ordered his mocha, he heard someone whistling across the room. It was Cayla, who motioned for him to join her.

Steve grabbed his mug and moved toward Cayla. She disappeared behind a bookcase, but he followed the whistling and found her digging through a desk in her little office.

He was struck by how petite she was—he hadn't remembered her being so small. When she finally spoke, he realized why. Her voice was deep, rich, and full. It was hard to imagine that such a small person could have that much resonance in her voice.

"So," she began without looking up, "how did the assignment go?" She continued to search the drawer.

"I did the survey, and I think it underscored what you said yesterday about people not being mind readers. I'm not sure where it's leading, but it taught me something."

"Like what?" Cayla asked as she pulled a pair of scissors from a tangle of rubber bands and paper clips.

"It wasn't so much the survey, but the discussion it generated," Steve clarified. "It became obvious that no boss can know and provide the motivation that every individual needs. Each of us has a different motivation for doing what we do, so it is up to us to take responsibility for creating a work environment that is motivating to us," Steve concluded confidently.

"Well done," Cayla said with a smile. "You have proved ready to take on the responsibility of self leadership. It's time to learn the first trick of a self leader." Cayla picked up her scissors and led Steve to a table nestled among the bookshelves. "What other insights did you have about being a self leader?"

"I don't know if this will make sense, because I usually need time to process things," Steve said.

"Go ahead," Cayla encouraged.

"It has to do with my whole way of thinking about the workplace—things I have believed since I started working, even as a kid. Up until yesterday, I thought my boss should know what I need and give it to me—but that's not how it works. I wonder what else I have wrong."

"Do you have a business card?" Cayla asked.

"Sure," Steve said, puzzled by her out-of-the-blue request. He pulled a card from his briefcase and handed it to her. "I apologize. I should have given one to you yesterday."

"It's not for me—it's for you. It's a challenge." Cayla held the standard-size business card in both hands, turning it over several times as though checking to be sure there was nothing abnormal about it.

She slid the scissors in Steve's direction and ceremoniously laid the business card down on the table. "Take these scissors and cut a hole from the card large enough to go around your head. By the way, a hole is a space surrounded by continuous paper—no gaps or breaks, or joining ends."

Steve looked at her as though she were crazy. Cayla sat silently, waiting.

"I know you said you were going to teach me some magic, but I don't have time for games, Cayla. My job is in jeopardy."

Undaunted, Cayla replied, "I know you think you don't have time for this. You can't imagine how it could be useful or relevant and besides, it's just a trick, right?"

"Now that you mention it, I hate parlor tricks—I've never been any good at them. I've lost more money in bars than you can imagine. Some people just have a knack for this kind of thing—I don't."

Cayla nodded. "Elephant thinking."

"Excuse me?"

"You've limited yourself based on your past experiences," she said, shaking her head in sympathy. "When they begin to train an elephant for the circus, they chain the baby elephant's leg to a pole in the ground. The baby elephant wants to get away. He pulls and tugs, but he can't escape—the chain is too big and the pole is too deep in the ground. So he stops trying. As he grows up, he just assumes he can't get away.

"Today he's a six-ton elephant. He could sneeze and pull out that chain—but he doesn't even try. Circus trainers say they can put a piece of string around that six-ton elephant's leg and he won't break away."

"So you're saying I'm like that elephant?" Steve frowned. "That because I've failed in the past I don't even try anymore?" Hearing the words out loud, he realized the impact of what he was saying.

Cayla smiled. "You have just tapped into the first trick of a self leader."

Steve perked up. "Really?"

"Yes. It's those kinds of assumptions that limit you every day. They're called ***assumed constraints.***"

"What's a consumed restraint?" Steve asked.

She laughed at his mangled terminology, then clarified:

*An **Assumed Constraint***

Is A Belief You Have,

Based On Past Experience,

That Limits Your

Current And Future

Experiences.

"Okay, I understand that I have assumed constraints about this scissors and card trick, but what's that got to do with my work situation?" Steve asked.

"You are assuming that you know what Rhonda, your team, and your client think and feel. You are assuming that you can't be successful in your role at work. You need to knock it off," Cayla said none too gently.

"This is depressing," Steve said.

"It could be inspirational," Cayla countered.

"Too bad I don't have your powers of observation. Then I'd know what everybody is thinking and I wouldn't jump to assumed constraints so often," Steve said.

"Being able to read people is a gift—but the greater gift is to know your *own* mind."

Steve winced. "Yeah. That's a definite challenge."

Cayla nodded. After a pause she said, "I have to go, but while we're on the subject of challenges, are you ready to cut a hole from your card big enough to go around your head?"

Steve took the scissors and picked up the card. To his astonishment, his business information was no longer on the card. Instead were the words:

The First Trick of a Self Leader:

Challenge

Assumed

Constraints!

He glanced up to commend Cayla on her sleight of hand, but she was gone. With an amused smile, he shook his head. Looking at his watch, he realized he should be going, too. In less than an hour he was due at the office for his dreaded team meeting.

❖ ❖ ❖

Steve arrived at the agency just in time to do some last-minute preparation. He'd been procrastinating, not sure how to tell the team members that their efforts had been rejected by the client. He knew they would look to him for answers, and he didn't have any.

The team—the creative guys, production coordinator, and media buyer—filed into the conference room to hear what United Bank had thought of the presentation. They must have sensed it wasn't good news. Without much chatter they took their places and waited for Steve to begin the meeting.

Steve began slowly. "United Bank acknowledged and appreciated the hard work that went into the campaign."

Peter, the Art Director, interrupted. "You don't have to butter us up, Steve. They must not have bought it or you would have said something before now. What did they say?"

Prompted by Peter's directness, Steve blurted, "They said it was garbage." Even Peter had no comeback.

Steve spoke into the silence. "I think we all would agree that it wasn't our best work. I don't have any answers right now, but I do have an apology."

He saw them sit up a little straighter as he continued. "My presentation was fine, and the effort you gave was fine. What didn't work was the lack of an agreed-upon budget and overall strategy. You can't create something in a vacuum—and for that, I take responsibility."

"Well, they aren't the easiest people to work with," Maril, the media buyer, offered.

Alexa, half the Peter and Alexa creative team, pretended to pull her hair out, saying, "They're bankers! What do they know about creative work? They probably wouldn't know good creative work from a hole in the ground!"

Steve was floored by the team's comments. All this time he had assumed their disdain was for him, when actually it was the client they had issues with. He was relieved until he realized that their perceptions came from the negative energy he'd shown toward the client. If they were down on the client, that was his responsibility. His assumed constraints had limited the whole team. How could he open their minds?

Suddenly, he had an idea.

He rummaged through his briefcase and found the scissors he'd taken from Cayla. He passed out a business card to each team member and said, "What if I asked you to cut a hole from my business card large enough to stick my head through?"

They stared at him.

"A hole is a space surrounded by continuous paper," he elaborated. "The paper must be one piece— no cutting it in two and joining ends around my head."

After giving his words a few seconds to sink in, he challenged them. "What are you thinking right now? What's going through your head about what I've just asked you to do? Jude? Maril? Alexa? Peter?"

Peter spoke first. "My first thought is, 'What's this got to do with anything?' "

Jude, the production coordinator, stated with conviction, "I don't think it can be done."

Maril shook her head. "It can probably be done or you wouldn't be asking, but I certainly don't have the time to waste trying to figure it out right now."

Alexa jumped up, grabbed the scissors and a card, and started cutting concentric circles that fell out in a spiral. She seemed confident of her solution until she realized that she would have to cut the paper spiral to unravel it, and that would break the rules. In defeat she uttered, "I hate these puzzles, I can never figure them out."

Peter observed each person's response until the group all looked to him. Quietly he stood, took a card, and folded it in half lengthwise. He cut a series of narrow slits from the folded edge to within a hairsbreadth of the opposite side.

Next he turned the card completely around so that the open edges were facing him. Going the opposite direction, he cut more slits between the other slits, again stopping within a hairsbreadth of the opposite end of the card.

Finally, he slipped the scissors into the fold and cut carefully. The group watched in awe as Peter unfolded the card. He pulled the slits apart as wide as they would go, revealing a fragile paper ring. Carefully, he slipped the ring over Steve's head and around his neck.*

The team broke out in applause. Peter looked humbled—the first time Steve had witnessed that emotion in him.

"I'm an art director," Peter explained, "and a lover of origami—the ancient Japanese art of paper folding. I've done stuff like this since I was a kid."

Maril looked at Steve. "This has been very entertaining and all, but what's the point?"

Steve sat down, clasped his hands in front of him on the table, and said, "Elephant thinking."

"Okay, I'll bite," Peter said.

Steve told them the elephant story that Cayla had told him. "Four of us had elephant thinking when challenged to cut the card. 'It can't be done, I don't have time, I'm not good at these kinds of things.' Our assumed constraints limited our belief that the trick could be done. But it turns out that one of us did have an answer."

---

* For instructions on how to perform this trick, see the Appendix.

" 'Assumed constraint,' " said Alexa, repeating the phrase. "What's that?"

"It's a belief based on past experience that limits your current or future experience," Steve said. "I now realize that I gave up on the creative process because I assumed you and Peter should have all the answers. I gave up on Rhonda because I assumed she had given up on me. And I gave up on United Bank because I assumed they were nuts!" There. He'd spoken the truth.

Alexa let out a chuckle. "I'm not sure it's an assumed constraint to think the client is nuts. Maybe they are."

Steve felt uncomfortable when the team laughed at the client's expense. Not wanting to come off too heavy, he let them enjoy the moment before he said, "I'm not sure I've been fair to United Bank. I'd like to suggest that we all give them the benefit of the doubt. They've suffered because I haven't handled the situation well. If we lose them, the entire agency will suffer."

Jude looked at him with concern. "Do you really think we'll lose the account?" she asked.

"I don't know. When I tell Rhonda about their reaction to the presentation, my bet is we'll either lose me or the client."

"I've heard rumors that, uh, Grant was going to take over the account," Maril said haltingly. "How do you feel about that?"

Too stunned to answer, Steve sat for what felt like an eternity. He hadn't heard any rumors. He loathed the idea that people were talking about replacing him.

"How do you think I'd feel?" he finally mustered.

Maril spoke slowly, choosing her words carefully. "You've been so discouraged, disgusted, and frustrated—I thought maybe you'd be relieved."

Steve felt completely exposed. He was transparent—not just to Cayla, but to his coworkers as well. How did he feel? He tended to be a thinker, not a feeler. Cayla's words flashed in his memory:

The real gift is to know your own mind.

"I can see why you think I'd be relieved," Steve heard himself reply, "but I don't want to give up. I want to meet the challenge. I'm not sure where to start, except to ask for your forgiveness as I try to stop the ship from sinking."

"Steve," said Peter, "you know I don't care much for account executives—the best way to kill a creative idea is to run it past one of you guys."

Steve laughed, though he knew Peter was only half-kidding.

"But for the creative process to work," Peter continued, "artists need guidance and direction. That needs to come from you."

"Peter is right," Alexa said. "And the place to start is with the client. You've got to steer them in the right direction—even if they are difficult."

"You're right, of course," Steve said. "That's where I'll start. I'll get the budget issue ironed out and let you know what we decide."

"In the meantime, I have an idea," offered Maril. "We should collect the recent campaigns of competitors and advertisers who are similar to our client. Let's get smart about what everyone else is doing—even though we don't know what we're doing yet."

The last fifteen minutes of the meeting were filled with enthusiastic energy as they mapped out a plan. As they left the meeting room, each team member wished Steve luck. He would need it. What could he possibly say to the client to turn this thing around? He had challenged his assumed constraints with his team, but now what? He felt powerless.

4

Cycles of Power

Steve was up early the next morning, even though it was a Saturday. The pressure he felt wouldn't let him sleep. He knew he needed an escape, even if for only a few hours. With dawn breaking, he went to the garage and pulled the cover off the majestic motorcycle that was his pride and joy. He rolled the gleaming Harley out to the street, strapped on his helmet, and threw his leg over the saddle. He started the motor and reveled in the powerful sound. He would spend this day as a wheeled warrior.

He shifted into gear and headed off. Thundering along the road, he realized there were so many things he loved about motorcycling—the proverbial wind in his face was only a small part of it. As he contemplated the joys of riding, he felt a sense of mastery over what he realized was actually a pretty inept machine. After all, a motorcycle couldn't even stand up by itself. Steve loved the synergy of riding—the melding of man or woman and machine that gave capabilities and power to both that neither possessed separately.

The magic of the moment was interrupted when the bike started sputtering and slowing down. He pulled over to take a look. He had been off the bike for no more than a few minutes when he heard another cycle pull up. There's an unwritten code among bikers, so Steve knew it must be another biker stopping to see if he could be of service.

"Need any help?" The voice sounded familiar. He looked up from the wiring he'd been fiddling with and his jaw dropped open.

"Cayla?" he said, flabbergasted.

Cayla looked as surprised as Steve as she shook her head. "Wow, isn't this a coincidence?"

"Somehow I don't think so," Steve said.

"You know, when I met you at the café I thought you looked familiar, and now I think I know why. Are you a H.O.G.?" Cayla asked.

"Yeah, I am. But I haven't been to a Harley Owner Group meeting for months," Steve said.

"So how'd it go with your team yesterday?"

Steve gave her a noncommittal shrug.

"I'm guessing," Cayla continued, "but tell me if I'm wrong: Yesterday you took responsibility, challenged assumed constraints, and decided to fight for your job and the client. The problem is, you don't know where to begin. You feel powerless."

"There you go again, reading my mind!" Steve shook his head, not knowing what to believe. "But you're right. That's why I took time out for a ride."

Cayla looked at Steve's cycle. "What happened?" she asked.

"She died on me," he said. He tested the ignition but nothing happened. "I know I've got plenty of gas, so it's probably a bad battery or a fouled spark plug." He rummaged through his saddlebag, searching for a spare set of plugs.

"Let me help," Cayla said as she pulled a spare set from underneath her seat.

"Are you sure these aren't trick plugs?" Steve asked, only half-kidding.

Cayla seemed not to hear his comment. "It's a shame that help like this isn't more common in the real world, isn't it?"

Steve wasn't sure if Cayla was speaking of the real world outside of cycling enthusiasts, or the real world outside the strange one created every time he met her.

Cayla continued, "Listen, there's a dealer close by. Why don't you follow me over there, so you can replace the plugs I loaned you?"

"I didn't know there was a shop around here," Steve said.

"Yeah, Hal's Harleys—I've been going there for years."

"Hal's?" Steve recognized the name. "Hal's is legendary. I didn't know it was around here. Sounds like a good plan to me."

They fired up their engines and Cayla took the lead. Soon Steve was again immersed in the pure joy of riding, wondering why it gave him such a thrill. He was so engrossed in his own thoughts that he almost missed Cayla's signal as she took a left off the road. A few yards farther down they turned left again into the Harley-Davidson dealership. Before Steve could dismount, Cayla was standing beside him, helmet and glasses already off.

"Power." Cayla spoke the word in a resonant voice that evoked its meaning.

Steve was confused. "Excuse me?"

"Power," Cayla repeated. "It's why you love to ride."

Steve started to freak. "How did you know I was thinking about—"

"I'm a keen observer, remember? I've seen that look before—I've *had* that look before—where you are lost in the joy of riding and you're not quite sure why. Well, I know why. It's the power, the knife-edged control, and the independence that riding offers."

"I'm not sure I agree it's about power and control," Steve countered. "Riding is fun—pure and simple."

"When did you start riding?" Cayla asked.

Steve enjoyed reliving the story of his love affair with motorcycles. He told her about riding on the back of his dad's motorcycle, hardly able to wait until he was old enough to ride for himself. When he was thirteen, he'd talked his dad into buying him a small scooter. At sixteen, he'd made his first road trip, riding from Denver to the Nebraska state line with his younger brother.

"I loved the feeling of independence and freedom from all the rules and regulations I lived with in school," he said. "But I wasn't on a power trip."

"Maybe you should reconsider the way you define power," Cayla suggested gently.

Words began to flow through Steve's head: abuse, corruption, coercion, control, authority, manipulation, money, domination.

Cayla studied him closely. "Interesting," she said. "I imagine that most of the words you're thinking about are negative, because you've seen power misused so much."

Steve opened his mouth to comment, but Cayla threw out another question.

"Have you ever known someone who was in a powerful position, but you had no respect for them?" she asked.

Silly question, thought Steve, *of course I have.* In addition to a couple of executive types at work, he could add a number of politicians—as well as Roger from United Bank.

Cayla nodded as though agreeing with his unspoken thoughts. "Lord Acton wrote, 'Power tends to corrupt, and absolute power corrupts absolutely.' Steve, think about all the negative stereotypes we have about power today—it's a wonder anyone would ever want to be powerful."

"I guess you're right," Steve admitted. "But I'm not sure where you're going with this discussion."

"I think you are trying to avoid power and I'm trying to help you understand why."

"Wait a minute," Steve said, feeling more than a little defensive. "I've got a problem just because I don't think power is everything it's cracked up to be?"

"Stay with me here," Cayla encouraged. "We were discussing the concept of power. I'm suggesting it is the sense of power that you love about riding. The power of being one with the bike; the power that brings you a sense of control. When you ride, you feel free. Compare this feeling to the way you feel about your work right now."

Steve groaned. He was trying *not* to think about work for a couple of hours. And he sure didn't want to compare riding to work.

"Do you feel powerful at work?" Cayla challenged.

Being an account executive in charge of United Bank should have made him feel empowered and free to do great work. Instead he felt restricted—stifled by others' expectations of him, burdened by his lack of experience with creative types, confused by a difficult client, and threatened by people such as Rhonda who were in positions that allowed them to determine his fate. Right now he certainly didn't have the feeling of being one with his job.

"In fact, I feel powerless," he confessed.

"Why do you think you feel that way?" Cayla asked.

"Because I'm not in a position to get people to do what I want them to do," Steve replied emphatically.

"Are you sure?" Cayla strapped her helmet on the back of her bike and said:

*

Don't Buy Into
The Assumed Constraint
That Position Power
Is The Only Power
That Works.

*

As she led him into the shop, Cayla said, "I want to introduce you to some people I think you'll appreciate. They all have discovered that there are a lot of ways to influence others and achieve their goals. We'll start with Woody—one of the best parts managers in the country. Knows most of the part numbers by heart. It's amazing. Just watch."

They walked up to the parts counter and Cayla was greeted warmly by a gracious young man.

"Hey, Cayla! What can we do for you? The world treating you okay?" He extended a hand and smiled brightly.

Cayla gave him a hearty handshake. "Yeah! Or at least it *will* be if you'll get my friend here a set of standard spark plugs. And can you ask one of the boys to check his electrical system? The beast died a few miles from here, and I had to rescue him." Cayla gave Steve a "just teasing" jab in the arm.

The young man winked at Steve. "Bike's not dead, right? Just resting." He smiled back at Cayla, cupped his hands together, and yelled, "Joey, pull me a set of 32310–78As."

Steve did a double take. The young man hadn't even looked up the part number.

Cayla smiled mischievously and turned back to the parts counter. "By the way, Woody, I'd like to introduce you to Steve. Steve, meet Woody, Parts Manager Extraordinaire."

Woody pulled out an order form. "Glad to help you with the parts, but first let me give you my standard song and dance." At that, Woody stood at attention, cleared his throat, and in a rich baritone recited:

"I stand behind the counter
In a motorcycle store,
Sometimes I'm called a genius,
Sometimes I'm called much more.
Some questions are important;
Some questions aren't, but oh, my Lord,
I'm supposed to be an Edison
Combined with Henry Ford.
I claim I'm no mechanic
But when the job goes sick,
The mechanic comes and asks me
What makes the darn thing tick.
But life would be a pleasure
And I'd grin from ear to ear
If the customer'd only tell me
The model, make, and year."

Steve laughed and promptly gave Woody the requisite model, make, and year.

As he completed the order form, Woody called out to the parts man behind him, "I'll also need a 32591–80 and a set of 31986–65Cs. Thanks, Joey."

Steve was impressed. "That's quite a skill you have there. How did you memorize all those part numbers?"

"Oh, there's a method to the madness. Once you understand the underlying principles behind the numbering system, it's not that hard."

Woody pointed at Cayla. "Actually, she's the one who helped me realize that knowing the system and part numbers is an important *point of power.* It's really helped me build credibility in this industry. I've had a terrific career, and I don't even have a tattoo!"

Cayla cast a sideways glance at Woody and he laughed. "Okay, I do have one small tattoo. Can't get anything past her!"

"What do you mean, 'point of power'?" Steve asked.

"A lot of people think there's only one kind of power—position power—and if you don't have it, you're a puppet of those who do," Woody explained.

"I've heard that before," Steve said as he winked at Cayla. "That kind of thinking is very limiting, isn't it?"

"It sure is! The best way to explain that is to demonstrate how we use points of power around here," Woody said. "Come on." He waved for them to come along as he led them to the service area.

Steve was enthralled by the hubbub of activity: mechanics joking, complaining, carrying on; cycles being rolled and towed and lifted; roaring engines being tested; customers questioning, concerned and nervous about the prognosis.

Woody explained, "When people bring their bikes in here, it's not as though they're bringing their motorcycles to a service department. It's more like they're bringing a child to the emergency ward. Our wrenches—mechanics, as lay people call 'em— obviously have **knowledge power.** They are experts at fixing Harleys. But they've also got **personal power**—their ability to give assurance to people and make them feel comfortable with the work that needs to be done and the costs involved. Cayla helped everyone understand that their personal power helps balance their knowledge power. That combination has made us incredibly successful."

With that comment, one of the sweaty and soiled mechanics called over from his workbench:

"Before Cayla worked with us, no one thought mechanics had much personality, let alone personal power! But look at us," the mechanic said with a smile. "We're actually quite charming."

Everyone laughed, and Steve was just about to comment on their easy camaraderie when Cayla said, "These guys have great working relationships, don't they? Let's go meet Jim, head of sales. He has some interesting ideas about *relationship power.*"

They found Jim in the showroom. As soon as Jim saw them, he walked over and gave Cayla a hug.

"Checking up on us, huh? Let me show you something!" Jim pulled a rumpled piece of paper out of his shirt pocket and proudly pointed to a list of numbers. "Look at these results from our latest customer sales and service report."

Cayla took the report from Jim and held it so that Steve could read along. "This is an incredible improvement over last time," Cayla noted. "What changed?"

Jim winked at Steve. "Cayla knows the answer, but I guess she wants you to hear it from me." He put his arm around Cayla's shoulders and gave a little squeeze. "Am I right?"

Cayla shrugged innocently.

"It's a little embarrassing," Jim began. "I've been in sales all my life, so I knew that relationships were vital. But somehow I got caught up in product information—I mean, it's easy to do when you love the product you're selling. With Cayla's help, I finally began to realize that I am good in sales because of my personal power—my people skills. People are my passion and I've built an incredible network. When I started to focus on those relationships, my sales and customer satisfaction increased. Sure, we sell and service Harley-Davidsons, but we're really in the people business."

"What exactly do you mean, 'focus on relationships'?" Steve asked.

"I began to realize that I had relationship power through my wonderful contacts—customers who were already happy with me and the dealership. I started cultivating those relationships and simply asking for leads. One relationship led to another. Now my problem is that I have all these great relationships and people who want to buy, and I have no motorcycles left! We've already sold out our annual allocation!"

"That's a nice problem to have," said Steve. "Let me ask you more about this relationship power. It's obvious how it works in sales, but how does it work in other parts of the shop?"

Jim discreetly pointed to a young woman working in the merchandise section of the showroom. "See the young woman by the leather jackets? That's Lisa, our apparel and accessories buyer. She's the daughter of the owner of the dealership. That's relationship power."

Steve frowned. "I'm not sure most people find nepotism a positive use of power."

"Ah," Jim said thoughtfully. "That's where most of us go wrong. We don't acknowledge our power because we're afraid of what others might think. But having power doesn't mean you have to use it. It certainly doesn't mean you have to abuse it.

"I can tell by the look on your face that you still don't agree," Jim continued. "When we first started discussing the issue of power here at the shop, Cayla asked each of us to write down what we thought our points of power were. Lisa didn't have 'Dad' down on her list. We all told her she should. She protested. She said she wanted to succeed on her own merit, not just because she's the owner's daughter. She was very sensitive about it.

"You know what I told her? 'Fool! If my dad were the owner of the shop, I'd take advantage of it. You can talk to him and get information that the rest of us can't. If you use your relationship power to do a better job and help the shop, then that's using your power in a positive way and we'll all be grateful, not jealous or resentful.' "

"Lisa got the job because it's her dad's business," Cayla added, "but she keeps it because of her knowledge and personal power."

Steve nodded. It was something he'd have to think about.

"You don't have to agree with everything, Steve, just take it into account," urged Cayla.

"Speaking of accounts," Woody said as he grabbed Steve's arm again and led him down the hall. "Let me introduce you to Dee Dee, our bookkeeper—one of the most powerful people in the shop."

As they approached the bookkeeper's desk, Steve took the lead. "Nice to meet you, Dee Dee, and in what way are you powerful?"

Dee Dee either didn't notice or chose to ignore the hint of mockery in Steve's voice as she replied with confidence, "I used to think I was low person on the totem pole around here. I mean, my job is the only one that doesn't deal directly with motorcycles. Then Cayla helped me realize my *task power.*"

Jim jumped in. "Funny, I always knew Dee Dee really runs this joint. I mean, she's the one who cuts the paychecks every week, withholds taxes, pays expenses, invoices our customers, and handles complaints. But she didn't see herself as having any power!"

"I guess I always thought of power being held by someone like our owner—someone who has ***position power***."

"So did I," said Steve with a smile, "but now I understand that there are many forms of power."

"Acknowledging the power you have gives you a sense of control over your job and your choices. I really enjoy my work much more now, even though I don't have position power," Dee Dee said with certainty.

"Are you implying there's no need for position power?" asked Steve.

"I hope not!"

At the sound of the voice, they all turned around. Standing behind them was a middle-aged, well-built man with a ponytail down his back. The man extended his hand to Steve.

"Nice to meet you. I'm Hal, the owner of this shop, and I'm here to tell you that position power is a good thing to have. But I've learned a great lesson: The best leadership situation is where you have position power and never have to use it! Like money in the bank, even though you may never need it, it's nice to know it's there. Besides, it's better to have people work with you—not for you."

Hal pointed to a plaque on the counter. "This is our leadership credo," he said.

> **The only way in which anyone can lead you is to restore to you the belief in your own guidance.**
> **—Henry Miller**

"That credo must work," Steve said. "Hal's Harleys is legendary and now I know why—you have all kinds of self leaders around here."

"They sure do," said Cayla, "and one of the ways they have become effective self leaders is by understanding the five kinds of power." With that, she pointed to a poster on the wall:

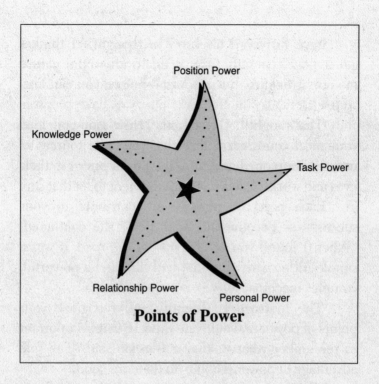

Points of Power

"As you can see," Cayla continued, "the first point of power is *knowledge power:* as Woody has; second is *personal power,* as the service reps have; third is *relationship power,* as Jim and Lisa have; fourth is *task power,* as Dee Dee has; and fifth is *position power,* as Hal has."

Steve furrowed his brow in thought. "I think I get it now," he said. "You need to know the nature of your strengths—your power—before you can lead yourself."

"That's right!" Cayla said. "How can you lead yourself if you don't realize that you *have* sources of power? Everyone has different types of power in their lives and work." Cayla paused a moment to let that sink in. "Each point of power can contribute to your success—or become the weak link," she continued. "When I found you on the side of the road, it was a simple little spark plug that had disabled a powerful, complex machine.

"The message is: Identify and recognize your points of power and cultivate them. But it is important to remember what Balthazar Gracian said, 'The sole advantage of power is ability to do more good.' "

"That's the first time I've ever heard power discussed as a tool for doing good," Steve confessed.

Cayla nodded knowingly. After another pause she asked, "How can you do more good for yourself, your family, your team, your organization, or your community if you don't have power?"

"I see your point," said Steve.

As they headed to the exit, Steve realized he'd been to dozens of motorcycle shops, but had never enjoyed hanging around one as much as he had this day. It wasn't just the hardware, noise, activity, and smells he loved. He realized it was the people he really enjoyed. These were enthusiasts, folks who loved what they did every day. They were people who had a sense of their unique points of power.

As he passed the parts counter, Steve waved good-bye to Woody.

"Don't forget your parts!" Woody said, pointing to a brown paper bag sitting on the counter.

"Oh yeah, thanks. And speaking of thanks, where'd Cayla go?" Steve asked as he looked around the showroom.

Woody glanced around and shrugged his shoulders. "Don't know," he said as he put the receipt in Steve's bag. "Hey, it was great to meet you! Ride safe!"

Outside the shop, Cayla's motorcycle was gone. Steve reached into his bag for the replacement parts and pulled out what he thought was the receipt. But instead it was a paper slip with a printed message:

The Second Trick of Self Leadership:

Celebrate Your

Points of Power

Steve shook his head in wonder. Was there no end to Cayla's tricks?

He fired up his big V-twin and notched it into first gear. As he roared away, he could hear Cayla's voice in his mind:

Perhaps your greatest weakness is not realizing your own power.

He would think about that later, when he figured out what to do about his job. For the moment he didn't want to think—he just wanted to ride. No, he *needed* to ride. It made him feel powerful.

5

Diagnose Yourself

Bright and early Monday morning, Steve headed for Cayla's Café, determined to save his job and keep his client. If Cayla couldn't help him, maybe the caffeine would. He'd spent Sunday poring over his files, notes, and proposals, looking for the flaw that had caused the client to reject the plan. In the process he realized that the only point of power he had with United Bank was task power. To restore the client's confidence, he would need knowledge power—and for that, he needed help.

Steve entered the café, keeping an eye out for Cayla. He made his way to the coffee counter, and just as he was about to ask the barista if Cayla was in, Steve heard the whistling. He turned around and sure enough, she was sitting at "their" table, as though waiting for him. Steve smiled and went over to join her.

"Where did you disappear to on Saturday?" Steve asked. "I still had questions."

"I thought you needed to be alone to process all you learned at Hal's," Cayla explained. "Where is your thinking now?"

"I've analyzed everything to death. I just can't figure out what's wrong with the budget and strategy I already proposed," Steve said with a sigh.

"Have you ever worked with a client to develop a comprehensive ad campaign before?" Cayla asked, though it was clear that she knew the answer.

"No, but I've drawn up dozens of budgets over the years, and the budget is the centerpiece of the strategy," Steve said in his own defense.

Cayla pulled out two rubber bands. "Steve, I'm going to use a magic trick as a metaphor for your situation. Will you play along with me?"

Steve shrugged his shoulders. "I guess so. If you're going to teach me that cool trick you showed the kids the other day, then yeah."

"I once met an old Indian mystic—" she began. Cayla the mentor transformed before Steve's eyes into Cayla the magician. She wove her story as she had before. Picking up the rubber bands, she demonstrated what appeared to be magic. She separated the tangled bands from each other as though moving matter through matter.

Knowing what was coming, Steve tried to detect the trick. But Cayla's performance was flawless. He found himself as delighted as the children had been— not because it was magic, but because he appreciated the skill behind her performance.

"Amazing!" he said.

Cayla reveled in his praise for a moment before switching back to her mentor persona. "Your goal, Steve, is to amaze someone with this magic trick by this time next week."

Steve laughed. He would enjoy sharing the trick with his girlfriend, Blair. He still hadn't told her what was going on at work. He knew Blair sensed something was wrong, but over the years she had learned to give him his space until he was ready to talk. It would be fun to lighten things up for her. "Okay, where do I start?"

"By asking yourself two questions about the goal of performing the magic trick: First, what is your level of competence? Second, what is your level of commitment? Let's start with the first question—your competence."

"I'm definitely competent!" Steve said confidently. "I watched you very carefully and saw exactly what you did, so I'm sure I can do it."

"So, if you are competent, take these and do the trick." Cayla handed him the rubber bands.

Steve took the two bands and entangled them the way he remembered Cayla doing it. He flexed and stretched the bands, attempting to separate them. The bands shot off his fingers and flew across the shop. Embarrassed, he stood to fetch them, but Cayla held her arm out and stopped him.

"I thought this might happen," she said with a smile as she pulled a large bag of rubber bands out of her case.

"What did I do wrong?" Steve asked.

"You acted as though you had competence when, in fact, you didn't," Cayla replied.

"That's harsh," Steve accused.

"No, it's simply the truth, and you needn't be ashamed. Competence means you have the knowledge and skill to accomplish the goal or do the skill in question. If you've never done the trick before, then you can't possibly have knowledge or skill. You are at the learning stage. What's wrong with that? You can't expect to be competent on a trick you've never done and have no idea how to do."

Steve nodded that he understood. "Okay, show me how."

Cayla took two rubber bands and placed them strategically on the thumb and index finger of each hand. She performed the trick slowly and deliberately.

Steve shook his head in admiration. "I think I get it now, but I suppose I'll have to practice before I'm actually competent. By the way, you said I was supposed to ask myself two questions about the goal. The first question was about my level of competence, but I forget the second one. What was it again?"

"The second question is, what is your level of commitment? Commitment is measured by your motivation and confidence about the goal," Cayla explained.

"When we started I was motivated and confident. Now I'm not so sure! I thought the trick would be easier than it's turning out to be," Steve said honestly.

"That's exactly what happens as you move through the development continuum!" Cayla said enthusiastically.

"The what? Are you taking me into a space-time continuum magic thing?" Steve joked.

"The development continuum is simply a model of four stages people usually experience when they are learning to master something." Cayla reached into her magic case and pulled out a laminated card, which she handed to Steve.

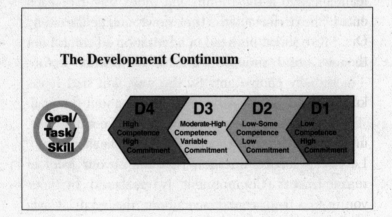

The Development Continuum

Goal/Task/Skill	D4	D3	D2	D1
	High Competence High Commitment	Moderate-High Competence Variable Commitment	Low-Some Competence Low Commitment	Low Competence High Commitment

"In terms of the rubber band trick, look at these four stages and tell me where you think you started and where you are now." Cayla's eyes were bright, as though she were about to reveal a great secret.

Steve studied the graphic and pointed to the square on the right. "I guess I started here, at D1, with low competence but high commitment. I moved to D2—low competence with low commitment—pretty quickly though, didn't I?"

Cayla leaned over the table to peer at the card. "That's normal," she said. "When you first begin to learn something or take on a goal, you have this naïve enthusiasm that overshadows your lack of competence. Once you get into the goal and realize you don't have the competence, your expectations are shattered."

"Reality shock," Steve said, nodding his head knowingly.

"Exactly!" Cayla seemed pleased with Steve's understanding. "D2, which is short for Development Level 2, is a natural stage of learning. It's where you realize there is a discrepancy between the expectations you had in the beginning—Development Level 1 or D1—and the reality of the current situation."

"So, everyone goes through this reality shock every time they are learning to do something?" Steve asked skeptically.

"The Development Continuum captures what people typically experience, so they can be better prepared to handle what will probably happen. It helps you recognize how your competence and commitment change as you learn something new or pursue a goal. Significant research validates these stages of development, but if you simply think about the goals you've accomplished—and ones you haven't—you'll realize your own experience is proof enough," Cayla said.

Steve picked up two more rubber bands as he reflected on Cayla's words. He entwined the bands, making sure they were placed on his fingers and thumbs the way he'd seen Cayla do it. He stretched and twisted them for show, then attempted to do the sleight of hand that would separate them as if by magic. Again, one of the bands went flying—almost hitting Cayla in the forehead.

Steve would have laughed if he hadn't been so mortified that he'd nearly poked out Cayla's eye.

"Okay. Stop, right there." Cayla held up both hands. "How do you feel about the trick now?"

"Frustrated, discouraged, disappointed," Steve said.

"That's why the second development level, D2, is called the Disillusioned Learner stage."

"What are the other stages called?" Steve asked.

"The first development level, D1, is called the Enthusiastic Beginner stage. That's where you began. If you make it through the second level, the D2 or Disillusioned Learner stage—where you are now— then you reach D3, which is known as the Capable But Cautious Performer stage. Finally, when you are a self-reliant achiever, you reach D4 or the High Achiever stage." Cayla pointed to each square as she described it.

"Excuse me, Cayla, but you said *if* I make it through the second stage of the Disillusioned Learner, then I go to the third stage of Capable but Cautious Performer. What happens if I don't make it?"

"You tell me," Cayla said.

Steve reflected a moment. "That's where I give up and quit, right?"

"Right," Cayla confirmed. "So, that's your dilemma on the magic trick right now, is it not? You realize it is going to take practice to master it, and you're not sure it's worth it. Am I right?"

"As usual."

"So quit."

"I just might." Steve sounded like a little boy defying his mother.

"It's always your choice to quit or keep going," Cayla reminded him. "But sometimes you give up without conscious choice, so it feels like failure."

"Are you suggesting that if I choose to quit then it's not failure?"

"When you are at the Disillusioned Learner stage of your goal and you lack competence and commitment, you are not a failure if you *thoughtfully* decide it is not worth the time and effort to proceed," she said. "You are a self leader taking responsibility."

"What if I don't want to quit?" Steve asked.

"I'll answer that question next time. That's the end of your lesson for today," she said with finality.

Steve couldn't hide his disappointment. "My lesson? What is my lesson? I've learned that I'm at the second stage of Disillusioned Learner on the magic trick and I'm about ready to quit my job—and that's my lesson?"

"Your lesson is to think about what it will take for you to get to the next level of development," Cayla gleefully announced as she headed toward her office.

Steve followed, feeling a sense of déjà vu at the now familiar scene of Cayla riffling through files and drawers to find what she wanted.

"Here it is." She handed Steve a crumpled sheet.

When I am at D1, the **Enthusiastic Beginner** level of development, with Low Competence and High Commitment, I need:

_____

_____

When I am at D2, the **Disillusioned Learner** level of development, with Low to Some Competence and Low Commitment, I need:

_____

_____

When I am at D3, the **Capable But Cautious Performer** level of development, with Moderate to High Competence and Variable Commitment, I need:

_____

_____

When I am at D4, the **High Achiever** level of development, with High Competence and High Commitment, I need:

_____

_____

"Your homework assignment is to write down what you would need to help you progress from Enthusiastic Beginner to High Achiever on this rubber band trick," Cayla said. "Remember, I want you to amaze your family and friends with it by this time next week."

"What do you mean, what I would need?"

Cayla stopped dead in her tracks. "Excellent question." Cayla slapped her open hand to her forehead. "I can't believe I forgot!" She grabbed the sheet from his hand and turned it over to reveal two columns on the back. Steve was puzzled. He could have sworn the back of the sheet was blank when she first handed it to him.

Pointing to the two columns, she said, "These are examples of what you need to increase your competence and build commitment if you are going to progress from Enthusiastic Beginner to High Achiever on a goal."

Steve turned the sheet over and over, still wondering how he could have missed noticing the two columns.

COMPETENCE	**COMMITMENT**
To increase your competence to achieve a goal, you need:	To build your commitment to achieve a goal, you need:

DIRECTION	**SUPPORT**
from someone who will:	from someone who will:

DIRECTION — from someone who will:

1. Set a clear goal
2. Generate an action plan
3. Show you how to do the goal or skill
4. Clarify roles
5. Provide timelines
6. Establish priorities
7. Monitor and evaluate your work and give feedback

SUPPORT — from someone who will:

1. Listen to you
2. Praise and encourage you
3. Facilitate your problem solving
4. Ask you for input
5. Provide rationale (remind you why you're doing it)
6. Share information about their experiences relevant to the goal
7. Share information about the organization relevant to the goal

"I hope this helps clarify what I meant," Cayla said. "When your competence is low, you need direction; when your commitment is low, you need support. If you can learn this, you'll know what you need and what to ask for at each development level."

"Fine, but once I know what to ask for—who do I ask?"

"That depends," Cayla said. "If it's about the magic trick, you can obviously ask me, other magicians, or even refer to a book on magic. What if it's about your United Bank ad campaign? Who do you ask for help on that?"

"Excellent question," Steve said. He felt as though he'd been jolted back into reality. He'd been so wrapped up in the magic trick and learning about the development continuum, he'd forgotten that the real point of it all was to save his job.

"Think of your goal for the United Bank account," Cayla said. "Think about the skills required to be an account executive and orchestrate their ad campaign. Then diagnose your development level on each of them. Remember:

*

When Your

Competence

Is Low, You Need

Direction;

When Your

Commitment

Is Low, You Need

Support.

*

"I think I've got it!" Steve said as he gave Cayla a high five and gathered his papers. He was eager to complete his homework and see how his new knowledge applied to his job.

6

Getting What You Need

It wasn't until later the next day that Steve finally had time to focus on Cayla's homework. He wrote out the answers to the questions, using the Competence and Commitment columns as a guide.

- *When I am at **D1**, the **Enthusiastic Beginner** level of development, with Low Competence and High Commitment, I need:*

  High Direction and Low Support

- *When I am at **D2, the Disillusioned Learner** level of development, with Low to Some Competence and Low Commitment, I need:*

  High Direction and High Support

- *When I am at **D3, the Capable But Cautious Performer** level of development, with Moderate to High Competence and Variable Commitment, I need:*

  Low Direction and High Support

- *When I am at **D4, the High Achiever** level of development, with High Competence and High Commitment, I need:*

  Low Direction and Low Support

Steve confirmed that he was at the Disillusioned Learner stage with the rubber band trick—he knew more than when he started, but still couldn't perform the trick and wasn't sure he ever would.

Now Steve was ready to apply the development levels to his own job. He began by listing what he had been responsible for when he was Rhonda's assistant: production budgets, media budgets, and production schedules. He diagnosed that his development level at that time had been the same in all of those areas, and that his needs had also been the same on each:

> *Goal:* Prepare and deliver production budgets, media budgets, and production schedules for Rhonda's accounts within expected timelines.
>
> *My Development Level:* D4—High Achiever
>
> *I Needed:* Low Direction and Low Support

In the past he had talked to Rhonda about her account and formed it into a budget for production or media. He had also taken her input and created production schedules. "Piece of cake—I was at D4 on all the above," he said aloud. But that was then. Now he didn't even have the confidence to do the things he used to take for granted. He made a note: *Used to be a D4—but I think I've gone backward!*

He turned his attention to what was happening now and asked himself: *What goals and tasks am I responsible for as an account executive for the United Bank account?* It was then that he had his "aha" moment. His role with United Bank now was very different from his role when he worked with Rhonda— yet he'd considered them the same. There was a big difference between preparing a budget based on Rhonda's input and having to develop one from scratch. He didn't have any idea where to begin—let alone how to sell United Bank on it. Considering the current circumstances, he acknowledged his new goal:

Goal: Get buy-in from United Bank for production budget, media budget, and production schedule
My Development Level: D2—Disillusioned Learner
I Need: High Direction and High Support

As he continued, Steve began to see a pattern:

Goal: Provide creative team with positioning and content statements
My Development Level: D2—Disillusioned Learner
I Need: High Direction and High Support

Goal: Provide media buyer with demographic targets, budget, and buying strategy
My Development Level: D2—Disillusioned Learner
I Need: High Direction and High Support

Steve shook his head in dismay—no wonder he was about to lose the account. He needed high direction and high support and he had gotten neither. He wondered if this was the third trick of self leadership.

Suddenly the phone rang and jolted him into the present. It was Marsha from accounting, reminding him that they needed his invoicing forms before the end of the day. "No problem," Steve said, even though it was.

Steve pulled out his accounting file. This is one area where he knew he was at D3—the Capable But Cautious Performer stage. He had high competence to complete the invoicing forms, but his commitment was variable. He was confident he could complete the forms; he just had no motivation to do it.

I Need: Low Direction and High Support.

He looked back at Cayla's list to see which of the supportive behaviors might stop him from procrastinating. Was there someone or some way to keep him from turning forms in at the last minute? What could he do to overcome his belief that this was nothing more than bureaucratic busywork? Again, questions for Cayla.

Steve finally completed the paperwork and dropped it off to accounting, hoping no one would notice it was late. It was long past 5:00 P.M., but he had one last bit of business: to clear his voicemail.

"You have one new message and three saved messages," the familiar recording announced. Steve pressed "3" to listen.

"Steve, this is Rhonda. We need to talk. I just picked up a message from Roger at United Bank and he is not pleased. I understand the proposal didn't go well. It would have been nice to hear it from you instead of the client. This sounds serious. Meet me at Irma's Eatery for lunch at noon on Monday. I told Roger I'd handle it, but you need to bring me up to speed. Bring me a copy of the original proposal. See you Monday."

Steve hung up and sat down. He had hoped for more time to put a comprehensive plan together. Now he had just three business days. At least he'd made progress. He'd taken responsibility for what happened at United Bank. He'd broken through his assumed constraints that the fault was with the client and creative team. He had acknowledged his task power and his need for more knowledge power. He had diagnosed himself at D2—the Disillusioned Learner stage—with low to some competence and low commitment on major aspects of the project. He knew he needed high direction and high support. Finally, he knew there were areas of the project where he used to be at D4—the High Achiever stage, but now he realized he wasn't sure about his commitment.

What he hadn't done was figure out what to say to Rhonda and how to save the account. Now he had only until noon on Monday to decide if he would hand in his resignation or fight to keep his job. He thought he was through blaming Rhonda, but he felt the anger rising again. She held his fate in her hands and he didn't know if he could trust her or not.

❋ ❋ ❋

Steve couldn't believe it was already Friday. Where had the rest of the week gone? Homework in hand, he headed back to Cayla's Café. He found her sitting at their table, reading a magic book. It was as though she'd anticipated his needs once again.

Barely glancing up from the book, she asked, "How'd you do on your homework?"

"I was hoping the teacher would check my work." Steve used a lighthearted tone that he hoped would cover the tension he felt.

"What's wrong?" Cayla asked.

"Whew, you're scary." Steve meant it as a compliment. "Rhonda left me a message. Roger from United Bank called her, none too happy. She's meeting me on Monday to 'discuss the account.' " Steve drew quotes in the air to emphasize the last three words.

"Sounds as though we'd better speed up your learning cycle," Cayla said as she cleared the table. "Do you have the laminated card I gave you that shows the development continuum?"

Steve found the dog-eared card in his notebook and handed it to Cayla.

Cayla tore the card in half.

"What are you doing?" Steve said, trying to keep his voice down.

Cayla stacked the two halves together and tore them in two.

"Oh, a trick?" Steve allowed.

Cayla took the four pieces and put them in the palm of her left hand. She laid her right palm on top, encasing the torn shards of paper between her two palms. She then raised her hands in prayer position and rubbed her palms back and forth as though grinding the pieces together.

"If this comes out in one piece, I'm going to freak," Steve said, more to himself than to Cayla.

Sure enough, when Cayla opened her hands, one piece of paper fell to the table. Her eyes met Steve's and looked back down at the piece of paper, beckoning him to pick it up. Steve tentatively took the paper, unfolded it, and gasped at the new image.

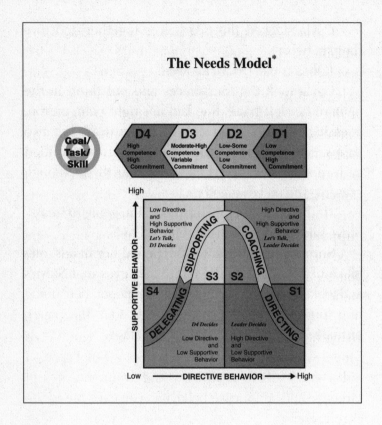

The Needs Model*

* See the full-color model printed on the inside cover of this book.

Cayla basked in Steve's awe for a moment before explaining. "This model will help guide you. For each development level, there is a corresponding leadership style to provide you with the appropriate amount of direction and/or support you need. At the D1—Enthusiastic Beginner stage, you need an S1 leadership style: ***Directing.*** At the D2—Disillusioned Learner stage, you need an S2 leadership style: ***Coaching.*** At the D3—Capable But Cautious Performer stage, you need an S3 leadership style: ***Supporting.*** At the D4—High Achiever stage, you need an S4 leadership style: ***Delegating.*** Pull out your homework and let's compare your answers with the model."

"I think I deserve high marks for this," Steve said, giving himself a verbal pat on the back. "The Needs Model will make it easy to remember, but I think I did a good job of figuring it out from the lists of directive and supportive behaviors you gave me to use as reference."

"Definitely an A plus," Cayla concurred after studying his work. "And you deserve special credit for understanding regression."

Steve was afraid he'd get marked down for not knowing what she meant, so he smiled as though he did. Cayla must have picked up on this, because she proceeded to explain what she meant.

"You picked up on the idea that you can be at the High Achiever D4 stage on something and regress backward to the Capable But Cautious Performer D3 stage," she said.

"Regression is a great word to describe what happened to me," Steve said. "I was at the D4—High Achiever stage on budgets and production scheduling when I worked with Rhonda. But I've become so discouraged lately that if she called me to do the same things I used to do, I'm not sure I'd have the confidence to do them. I've definitely regressed from the High Achieving stage to the Capable But Cautious Performer stage."

"Good diagnosis," Cayla said, complimenting Steve. "You also seem to understand that in your new role as an account executive, you began at the D1—Enthusiastic Beginner stage, gathering information from the client, analyzing their needs, and generating a plan from scratch. But now you are at the Disillusioned Learner stage."

"It's embarrassing, but I was so naïve that I didn't know I was supposed to gather information from the client in the first place. I was enthusiastically trying to create plans from thin air! When it didn't work, I quickly moved to disillusionment."

"It's all a part of the learning process," Cayla said philosophically.

Steve sighed. "If I'd had the Needs Model from the beginning I could have worked with Rhonda to get my needs met. The question now is: Is it too late?"

"It's never too late to try," Cayla said. "I'm sure you'll find some answers this weekend as you prepare for your lunch meeting with Rhonda."

At the mention of the weekend, Steve realized he was already late for his Friday night dinner with Blair.

7

Running Together

Blair was waiting patiently when Steve arrived. He was relieved to see her, but feeling guilty. He should have called to tell her he was running late.

"Sorry to keep you waiting," he said as he gave her a heartfelt hug.

"I was afraid something happened," she said.

Steve heard genuine concern—not scolding—in her voice.

"You've been so busy we haven't gotten together all week. What's going on?" she asked.

"A lot," Steve replied.

"You okay?" she asked.

"Physically, yes," he said cryptically.

Over dinner at their favorite Mexican restaurant, Steve shared the strange events of the past week. He began with the botched ad campaign proposal for United Bank and how it led to meeting Cayla. He pulled out one of his business cards and asked Blair if she had a pair of scissors in her purse. She looked at him quizzically. Smiling mischievously, he asked her to cut a hole in the card large enough for him to put around his head.

"That's why you're upset? A strange woman asked you to cut a hole in your business card and stick your head through it?"

Steve laughed for the first time that evening, "Partly," he kidded. "Now, go ahead. Try it."

"It's a trick." Blair refused to pick up the scissors.

"You're absolutely right!" Steve said with enthusiasm. "Actually, it's the first trick of a self-leader." He told her about elephant thinking and the importance of challenging assumed constraints. He then took the scissors, cut the card into a large ring, and placed it over her head. The people at the next table—who'd been stealing glances their way—clapped in appreciation.

"Okay," Blair said, "so what did you do with this revelation about assumed constraints?"

Steve described the meeting with his team, where he'd realized that his assumptions about his team members, the client, and his role had made him a victim. "I'm not exactly a natural-born leader," he said with a shake of his head.

Blair reached out and touched his hand. "Is that why I didn't see you last weekend—because you're feeling down on yourself? Did your motorcycle ride help at all?"

"I almost forgot about that, and it's the strangest part yet."

"What happened?" Blair asked.

Steve told her how his Harley had mysteriously died, and about his bizarre roadside meeting with Cayla. He described the trip to the legendary Hal's Harleys dealership, the conversation about power, and the mysterious "receipt" revealing the second trick of self leadership.

"So what's the trick?" she asked, sounding both curious and skeptical.

Steve handed the receipt to her.

" 'Celebrate your points of power,' " Blair said, reading from the slip of paper.

"I certainly didn't use my points of power with the United Bank account project," Steve said. "I should have been the one initiating action and directing others."

"But how could you lead others when you didn't even know what you were doing? You've never been an account executive before." Blair's statement surprised Steve. How could it be so clear to her, when he had needed Cayla to point it out to him?

"I finally realized that today. I think I'm in the midst of learning the final trick. At first I diagnosed myself at the D1—Enthusiastic Beginner stage on almost every aspect of my role, but because I didn't get the S1—Directing leadership style I needed, I'm now at the D2—Disillusioned Learner stage, and I need an S2—Coaching leadership style. On some things, such as budgeting and scheduling, I was at the D4— High Achiever stage and fine with an S4—Delegating leadership style. But now I'm not sure I'm as competent as I thought, so I've regressed to the D3— Capable But Cautious Performer stage, requiring an S3—Supporting style of leadership." The words tumbled from Steve's lips without pause.

When he was finished, Blair was staring blankly at him. "I have no idea what you just said."

Steve roared with laughter. "I must sound like I'm speaking a foreign language. Wait just a second." Steve rose from the table and disappeared around the corner. When he returned, he had two rubber bands that he'd managed to get from the restaurant's front desk.

"I was talking about the four stages of learning something new," he said. "I'm going to show you a rubber band trick as an example." He began teaching Blair the magic trick, pulling out the laminated card with the Needs Model and using it for reference.

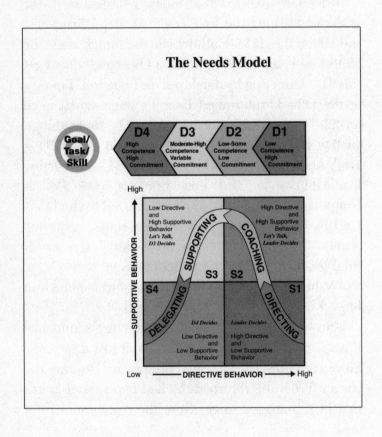

After a few minutes, they decided they were both at D2 on the rubber band trick.

Blair's eyes grew bright as she saw the connection between the rubber band trick and Steve's work.

"So as far as your job goes, you've diagnosed yourself at the D2—Disillusioned Learner stage on most of your important goals, and you've determined that you need more direction and support to succeed in your job." Blair frowned. "So where do you go from here?"

Steve confided that he had until noon on Monday to figure it out. "I'm not sure if I should resign and end the pain or fight for my job and risk having Rhonda fire me. What do you think?"

"I think you are very lucky to have run into Cayla," Blair said. "I'll make you a deal. If you'll help me with my 10K run tomorrow, I'll help you think through a plan for your meeting with Rhonda."

"Oh, man! I've been so wrapped up in my own problems I forgot you have your first race tomorrow." Steve shook his head. "I want to help, but I'm not sure what I can do between now and tomorrow morning."

"Here's my diagnosis," Blair said, referring to the Needs Model. "When it comes to my training schedule, I'm capable of the short runs during the week. But I'm never confident that I'll finish that 10K practice run on the weekend. I think I'm stuck at D3—the Capable But Cautious Performer stage. For the race tomorrow I'm at the D2—Disillusioned Learner stage. I've never run in a race with hundreds of people before, so my competence is low. I don't know how I'll react and I'm afraid. Guess that means my commitment is low. What if I can't finish?"

"Come on, Blair," Steve encouraged. "You can *walk* six miles if you have to."

"What if I come in last? I'll be horrified." Blair put her hands over her eyes as though trying to block out the sight of her straggling in in last place.

Steve laughed. "You *are* a Disillusioned Learner! How can I help you?"

"I've got an idea." Blair's mischievous smile made Steve wonder what he'd gotten himself into. "I have relationship power with you, and I'm going to use it. Here's my request: Run with me. You've run in dozens of races and know what it's like. You have knowledge power. Be my running partner and coach. I need an S2—Coaching leadership style, with lots of direction and support."

"Are you kidding? I haven't trained," Steve complained.

"As slow as I am, you don't need training to keep up!" Blair said. "We can talk about it on the way home."

* * *

As the sun came up Saturday morning, Steve put on his running gear, did some quick warm-ups, and headed out the door to pick up Blair.

Blair beamed when she saw Steve in his running clothes. "I knew you'd go for it," she said as she handed him a bagel and a sport drink. "I had a feeling you might need this," she added a little smugly.

"I realized I couldn't turn down a self leader in need," Steve said with a smile. "You asked for help and that takes strength. It's hard to turn someone down who knows what they need."

"I've been thinking about that," Blair responded. "The two tricks Cayla taught you are potent. I wouldn't be a runner at all if I hadn't used them—I just wasn't aware I was using them."

"Explain," Steve urged.

"Remember when I first started running? I bought cute shorts and tops, running shoes, good socks. I had all the best stuff. I was feeling very proud of myself. I took off down the street, ran the first block, and began to feel my thigh muscles tighten. I tried to control my breathing, but I couldn't get any air. I got that side stitch that wouldn't go away."

Steve chuckled. "I remember your excuse. You said, 'I must have fast twitch muscles. They're not really built for long-distance running. Running isn't that good for my knees, anyway.' "

"I didn't whine like that!" Blair reached over and lightly shoved Steve. "Anyway, I wanted to quit. I started off at the D1—Enthusiastic Beginner stage and it only took me two blocks to get to the D2—Disillusioned Learner stage! Do you remember what you told me?"

Steve shrugged, "Remind me."

"You explained that running uses very different muscles than what I was used to. You told me it was going to require more effort than buying good shoes."

"I nailed that one," Steve said proudly.

"The interesting thing is, I used to be a pretty good sprinter and never thought I could run longer than a hundred yards. That was my assumed constraint."

"Not fast twitch muscles?" Steve chided.

Blair sounded a little defensive as she responded, "Maybe I did have fast twitch muscles, but that didn't mean I couldn't run ten kilometers."

"So what did you need?" Steve asked.

"I needed coaching," Blair responded. "I needed to learn to run differently. I needed someone to show me how. Someone to observe, monitor, and evaluate my running and give me feedback. When I started I needed an S1—Directing leadership style, but since I never got it, I was at the point where I needed an S2—Coaching style of leadership."

Steve was impressed. "I remember now. You went to a friend who was a high school cross-country coach and he helped you put a training program together."

"I used my relationship power to find someone with knowledge power," Blair explained. "He helped me map out an entire strategy that included a running support group, getting feedback on my breathing and running technique, subscribing to a running magazine, and having you lovingly hold me accountable for meeting my training schedule."

"I have a feeling this is leading to something other than your running," Steve said suspiciously.

"Don't you see? Think about it:

✿

When Goals Work Out,
It Is Usually Because
You Instinctively
Take The Initiative
To Be A Self Leader
And Get What You Need
To Succeed.

✿

"Exactly," Steve agreed. "And Cayla has revealed why some of our goals aren't reached—because our assumed constraints defeat us."

"It occurred to me that a big mistake we make in our jobs is thinking that the only place to get direction and support is from our managers," Blair said. "But as you realized with your team the other day, that's an assumed constraint. Steve, you have a number of people and resources you can tap into to get the direction and support you need to turn this United Bank account around. I have a feeling you have points of power you haven't begun to use." Blair paused for a moment before adding, "We need to map out a strategy for your meeting with Rhonda; just like I did with my running. I think it will work!"

She said it with such optimism that Steve's spirits were lifted. "If it doesn't work out, I can always fall back on my exit strategy and quit," he said.

Blair let out a heavy sigh. "I think quitting is just your way of feeling some sense of control in a frightening situation. For now, let's focus on today's goal."

Steve pulled into the parking lot, where hundreds of runners were congregated. "What *is* your goal today?" he asked. "What time are you trying to make?"

Blair laughed out loud. "My goal is: *Complete the annual charity 10K race.*"

"Fair enough. If just finishing the race is motivating enough, that's what we'll focus on doing. But I think you should set one standard," he said. Calling Blair's attention to what appeared to be an eighty-year-old woman, he declared, "I think you should try to beat her."

Blair didn't take the bait. "That's not a smart goal! I have no control over how fast that woman runs. It'd be just my luck that she holds the national title for senior women."

"Shouldn't you have *some* standard?" Steve asked in all seriousness.

"Okay, how about this: My goal is not to be the last one over the finish line. That means that if I can't continue, you have to carry me over!"

They made their way to the registration table, picked up their numbers, and pinned them on their T-shirts. All kinds of people milled around the booths that offered food, drink, products, promotions, and massages. Music filled the air. The atmosphere was electric and Steve felt energized. It was fun just being part of the event.

People were gathering at the starting line. Blair and Steve were positioned midway in the pack when Blair darted forward, weaving her way to the front. She turned back and signaled for Steve to follow her.

"She doesn't know the front of the pack is reserved for qualified runners and sponsored professionals!" Steve thought aloud. He wondered if she would notice that the numbers pinned to their shirts were in the range of 003 and hers was 2045. As she reached the front row, he realized she was too pumped up to notice much of anything.

"On your mark," the starter bellowed from the PA system. Steve hadn't reacted in time to stop Blair. "Get set." The shot of the starting gun rang out. They were off. The exhilaration he had at the start of a race thrilled Steve. He could actually feel the ground shaking from the thousands of feet pounding behind him. As he sprinted up to catch Blair he could hear the collective breathing of hundreds of runners. Within seconds they were passing by.

"Unbelievable!" Blair shouted. "Why are people running so fast this early in the race? I'll never finish if I try to keep up." She didn't know how to pace herself. "I'm already ready to give up! What should I do, coach?"

"Just make it to the fountain."

She smiled through her pain. "Okay, so I make it to the fountain, then what?" she asked, breathing hard.

"Feel the spray coming off the fountain. It's invigorating! And, remember your goal."

"Oh, yeah. Finish."

"What happened there at the start of the race?" Steve's question was more than a query. He hoped it would guide her to a realization.

"I got so excited—I decided to go for it! I thought maybe I could win my age group or something."

Steve found Blair's innocence endearing. "That would be something, wouldn't it? To win your age group in your first race, after training for a couple of months." He tried not to sound too judgmental.

Blair got it. "Oh, how embarrassing," she said between breaths. "I acted as though I were at the High Achiever stage—starting up front, thinking I could outpace or at least keep pace with the best. I was actually at the classic Enthusiastic Beginner stage! So that's why I'm back at the Disillusioned Learner stage. It didn't take me long to get from D1 to D2, did it?" She clearly didn't need an answer.

Steve replied anyway. "Remember the old Italian proverb: Things get harder before they get easier." It struck him that he needed to heed the adage himself. His frustration with his job, he noted, was a normal part of the learning curve that needed to be acknowledged and dealt with. It wasn't a reason to quit.

Soon they passed the fountain and felt the invigorating spray. "I made that milestone," Blair panted. "Now what?"

"Keep going, one step at a time," Steve replied.

For the rest of the race, Blair asked Steve for—and gave herself—as much direction and support as she could: *Just make it around the corner. Good girl. Now just make it up to those two people—they don't seem that fast. Way to go, Blair!* She encouraged herself out loud so Steve could add something if he thought she needed it. Every once in a while she asked Steve for specific directions. *Am I using my arms efficiently for uphill climbs? Do I need to do something different as we go downhill? If I'm breathing too hard to talk does that mean I'm pacing myself too fast and should slow down for a bit?* Sometimes Steve gave her direct answers; sometimes he asked her to experience it and report back what she thought was best.

An hour into the race, Steve was jogging easily. Such was not the case for Blair. She was huffing and puffing, almost wheezing.

At last they caught sight of the finish line. "Okay, coach," Blair managed to pant, "other runners have said this was where they get that rush of adrenaline—their second wind—and sprint for the finish. I don't have any hope—I'm not sure I ever found my first wind. My legs are like lead. My lungs ache. I hope I can finish."

Steve was really worried. He didn't want to carry her across. Then, they heard familiar voices cheering from the sidelines. They glanced over and saw a group of friends yelling and screaming like crazy.

"Oh, wow!" Blair said, "I didn't know they'd all be here!" She smiled despite the pain. "I'm sure they're in shock seeing that I'm still upright!"

"And that you're not last," Steve added with a wink.

With that, Blair's entire face and body changed. She caught her second wind. "Let's go!" she shouted, waving to their friends as she took off. Steve was just ready to kick it up a notch when he thought he noticed another familiar face in the crowd. Was that Cayla, cheering them on? No, it couldn't be. He looked again and the face was gone.

Blair beat him to the finish line. When he arrived, Blair hugged him jubilantly. "Thank you, thank you, thank you!" she bubbled. He hugged back but kept her walking, fearing her legs might cramp.

"Look!" Blair said, pointing toward the finish line, "People are still finishing!"

People were still coming in, but even more runners had finished before them. It had taken them just over an hour to run 6.2 miles. That was not a particularly fast time. At that moment Steve had an epiphany. He knew Blair was a very competitive person. Yet curiously, knowing that hundreds of people had finished before she did didn't bother her. In fact, she was overjoyed to finish the race—to have achieved her goal. It didn't matter what the others had done.

The race helped Steve realize:

❋

There Is Magic
In Diagnosing Your
Development Level
And Getting The
Direction And Support
You Need To Achieve
Your Goal.

❋

Without getting what she needed, Blair would have quit after fifteen minutes. Just as he was about to quit after a couple of months of being an account executive.

Soon they were surrounded by their friends. They spent the next hour collecting their new T-shirts and enjoying the booths, exhibits, and goodies that come with finishing the race. As they walked to their cars, Blair hugged each of their friends.

"You all gave me the support I needed, when I needed it," she said. "Thank you for reminding us that there are so many ways to get what we need—and friends are a great place to start."

Later, as they sat in the traffic line inching toward the parking lot attendant, Steve asked Blair to sort through the bag of coupons and free samples and find their parking ticket.

"Are you sure you put it in here?" she asked. "I can't find it."

They were at the parking lot pay booth. Steve hated holding up traffic. He rolled down the window to explain that they were still searching for the ticket. "Don't worry, it's taken care of," the attendant said.

"What do you mean?" Steve asked.

"That woman paid for you." The attendant pointed up ahead, where a small woman on a Harley-Davidson roared through the exit. "She said something about being proud of you," the attendant said as he handed Steve a receipt.

Steve thanked the attendant, handed Blair the receipt, and pulled onto the highway. "That was Cayla up ahead," he said in an amazed tone of voice. "I thought I saw her in the crowd, but figured I was seeing things."

"Did you tell her we'd be here?" Blair asked.

"I don't remember," Steve said.

"Well, this is no ordinary parking receipt," Blair said as she held it up for Steve to see. The receipt was emblazoned with the message:

The Third Trick of Self Leadership:

Collaborate

for Success!

8

No Excuses

Steve was a man with a plan, out the door at 7:00 A.M. on Monday. First stop: Cayla's Café. Instead of beelining it for the coffee counter, he immediately looked around for Cayla and found her sitting at the same old table.

"You have a lot of explaining to do, Cayla."

"Do I?" she said, arching her brows.

"I don't want to sound ungrateful, but my curiosity is killing me."

A waitress began to bus the table next to them, and Steve took a few moments to order coffee and scones for them.

"Okay, back to the explanations," Steve said.

Cayla met his gaze. "I'm quite sure you have many legitimate questions, but don't you think we ought to focus on the most important questions first? How are you going to handle your lunch with Rhonda? How are you going to save your job? How are you going to implement the plan you and Blair put together?"

"See? That's what I mean!" Steve said in a rising voice. "How do you know Blair and I put a plan together?"

Cayla made a palm-down motion. "Calm yourself. I saw the two of you during the race. It was a perfect example of collaborating for success. You are both very bright, so I just figured you would leverage your partnership and come up with a plan for today."

"Fine," said Steve. "Your great powers of observation and reasoning have worked again. But why were you there observing in the first place? I don't remember telling you about the race."

Again Cayla responded matter-of-factly. "I knew some other people in the race, and I was there to cheer them on. You might have noticed one of them— a wonderful lady. She's almost eighty and she's still running! Finished before the two of you, I might add."

"Glad Blair didn't notice that," Steve said under his breath.

"What was that?" Cayla asked.

"Nothing," Steve said with a half-smile. "I guess I jumped to conclusions. But you have to admit there have been an inordinate number of coincidences lately. Like our chance meeting near Hal's Harleys, for example."

"Life is full of pleasant surprises," Cayla said. "Look, you have only a few hours before your big meeting with Rhonda. What questions do you have about your plan?"

Steve pulled out the multi-page plan that he and Blair had created and handed it to Cayla. It was then that he realized they hadn't gotten their coffee and scones. As the waitress walked by, he caught her attention.

"Excuse me," he said abruptly. "Is our order on the way?" The waitress nodded and walked off.

Cayla was still concentrating on the plan, making little noises in apparent approval. Steve decided that her "uh hum's" were not enough, and decided to ask for feedback.

"Since I'm at the D2—Disillusioned Learner stage as a self leader—especially when it comes to my meeting with Rhonda—is it okay to ask you for more specifics?"

Cayla didn't respond immediately. She seemed to be weighing his question.

Fearing he'd blundered, Steve stuttered, "If you can't, I mean, if you don't want to give me feedback—"

Cayla put her finger to her mouth. "Watch," she whispered.

As the waitress walked by again, Cayla reached out to get her attention. "Excuse me. I need to ask you about our order. My colleague here is getting grumpy without his morning java!" she said with a smile.

"Oh, I know the feeling! Let me check." The waitress turned around and hurried back to the coffee counter.

"Thanks so much, Gail," Cayla called, oozing appreciation.

Gail returned a few seconds later with the coffee and scones.

"Must be your charming personality," Steve quipped. "She ignored me when I asked."

"Not charm—technique," Cayla explained. "I simply used the two most powerful words in the English language to get what I needed."

" 'Thanks, Gail'?" Steve ventured.

"That didn't hurt, I suppose. But that's not really what made the difference. Think about the way you addressed Gail versus the way I handled the situation."

Steve was thoroughly confused.

Cayla provided the answer. "I used the two most powerful words in the English language for getting cooperation."

Steve waited to hear what the two words were.

"*I need,*" Cayla declared.

"That's it?"

"Correct," Cayla said firmly.

"That's interesting, Cayla, but what does that have to do with you giving me feedback?"

"It's not that I don't want to give you feedback, it's just that there is a much more powerful way for you to get feedback from me. Don't ask."

Now Steve was totally lost. "But I thought I should be proactive as a self leader and ask for feedback."

"I said *get* the feedback—I didn't say *ask* for it. Let me be more precise. Don't put the request in the form of a question. In this case, playing *Jeopardy!* puts you in jeopardy." Cayla smiled at her play on words before reinforcing:

✷

The Two Most
Powerful Words
To Collaborate
For Success Are:
"I NEED."

✷

"As a self leader, it is your responsibility to get the feedback, direction, and support you need," said Cayla. "The problem is that instead of stating what you need in a direct, forthright manner—especially when you are at the D2—Disillusioned Learner stage—you get trapped asking dumb questions."

"Like what?" Steve queried, fearing he'd just asked one.

"Here's a great example," Cayla said, full of enthusiasm. "A man got on the subway in New York City, and discovered that there was only one seat left. But there was something on the seat that he didn't want on his slacks, so he laid his newspaper down and sat on it. A few moments later a woman tapped him on the shoulder and asked, 'Excuse me, sir, are you reading your newspaper?' The man thought that was one of the dumbest questions he'd ever heard. He couldn't help himself. He stood up, turned the page, sat back down on the paper, and replied, 'Yes ma'am, I am.'"

Cayla laughed at her story. "That's the problem with a dumb question. You get a dumb answer."

Steve cracked up—more at Cayla than at her story. But he wasn't sure about this question thing. How could he ask for help without asking a question? Steve took a risk.

"Cayla, I hope this isn't another dumb question. But what makes a question dumb? Obviously not all questions are dumb. In fact, I've always heard that there's no such thing as a dumb question."

"Smart question," Cayla said. "There are three types of dumb questions. One, when the answer is obvious. Two, when you're not willing to hear a certain response. And three, when you already know what you want to hear.

"For example, Rhonda is running around with her head cut off, but you need some help. So you ask, 'Are you busy?' That's a dumb question. Of course she's busy! So she says something like, 'There just aren't enough hours in the day.' You feel guilty, so you get flustered and leave her alone so as not to add to her burden.

"It is better for you to just simply state your needs truthfully: 'Rhonda, I need fifteen minutes of your time to discuss this project. If this isn't a good time, I can come back at three o'clock.' "

Steve couldn't deny that he often asked what appeared to be the dumb question instead of stating his needs directly. "What makes the 'I need' phrase so powerful?" he asked.

"When you tell someone you *want* something, their first thought is usually, *We all want things we can't have.* When you use the *I need* phrase, you're coming from a position of strength. You've thought about what it's going to take to succeed and are requesting a person's help. It's amazing, but human beings love to feel needed. They love to think they can help you. 'I need' is very compelling."

"All right. I'll try not to ask dumb questions. But I reserve the right to ask smart ones," Steve said. "How's this: I *need* specific feedback on my plan so I can get what I need to make it work."

Cayla complied immediately by turning her attention to Steve's neatly printed plan. After reading it over, she summarized:

"You **challenge assumed constraints,** the first trick of self leadership, by listing potential and actual assumed constraints that could limit your success on the United Bank account. The way you turned your assumed constraints around is very effective. I especially liked this one: 'My assumed constraint is that I think Roger is egotistical and won't listen to anything I say.' The turn-around statement: 'Roger is not egotistical and is open to my recommendations.'

"You **celebrate your points of power,** the second trick of self leadership, by highlighting your strengths and resources. But you've gone even one step further and identified other people who have points of power that you can draw upon as you implement your plan. You must feel good about that.

"And, finally, you have started using the third trick of self leadership—**collaborate for success**—by prioritizing your most important goals on the United Bank account, diagnosing your development level on each of them, and determining the leadership style you need."

For the next hour, Cayla helped Steve create an agenda for his meeting with Rhonda. Finally, it was time for Steve to go. He packed up the papers and took a last swig of his now cold mocha. Before he left, Steve reached over and gave her a big hug.

"This meant a lot to me today. I won't forget it—no matter what happens." He said the words with such sincerity that even he was surprised.

Cayla was visibly moved. She squeezed his arm and headed for her office. As Steve walked out the door, he heard her voice calling out:

"Don't get derailed by disillusionment!"

Steve smiled. Cayla always seemed to have the last word.

* * *

Time to work the magic, Steve thought.

He straightened his already straight tie and glanced in the rearview mirror to get a sense of himself before going into Irma's Eatery. He was a few minutes early. The last thing he wanted to do was to keep Rhonda waiting.

Briefcase in hand, he found the most private booth available and faced forward so he could catch Rhonda's attention when she entered. He pulled out his notes, the United Bank proposal, and his Palm Pilot. The waitress dropped off a glass of ice water.

"Thanks, Tina. I need another glass—someone will be joining me for lunch." Steve smiled at how well the little things worked. Tina was not only prompt, but attentive.

"Looks like an important meeting," Tina observed.

"Could be one of the most important in my career so far, as a matter of fact," Steve revealed.

"Is there anything I can do to make it go more smoothly?"

"Wow, that's really kind of you," Steve said. "Come to think of it, yes. If this is too much to ask, let me know. I need to stay focused, so rather than checking in on how we're doing and risk interrupting a delicate moment, I'd appreciate it if you wait for me to signal that we need something. Oh, and make sure you give the check to me."

"Consider it done." Tina gave the thumbs-up sign. "And good luck!"

Steve smiled. It felt good to have a collaborator for success.

Outside the window, a silver-gray BMW pulled into the parking lot. He watched as Rhonda gathered her things and made her way to the restaurant's entrance. Confident, poised, and energetic, Rhonda was someone Steve admired on general principle. He prepared himself for her direct, no-nonsense approach. She would pull no punches, get right to the point, and leave with a general plan of action. As nervous as he was, he realized how much he wanted to work with her—he had so much to learn.

He stood so she could spot him. She smiled. He observed that the smile was genuine, but restrained. He understood that she needed to hold back, given the seriousness of the situation.

Steve stepped out of the booth to greet her. They did a semi-professional half-handshake, half-hug hello. After Rhonda sat, so did Steve.

Typically, Steve would wait for Rhonda to speak. He would listen, formulate an opinion, and then decide how or if to respond. But this was a time to be bold, so before Rhonda began, Steve launched the first volley.

"Rhonda, I know you cut your trip short because of this meeting. You expressed disappointment that you heard about the outcome of the presentation from Roger and United Bank before you heard from me. I'm not going to give you excuses. I think your disappointment is warranted. I'm here to bring you up to speed with what I know and listen to what you think. But, I also need you to know that I've done my homework. I have ideas for moving forward and I trust you'll be open to discussing them."

"What kind of ideas?" Rhonda asked, cutting to the chase.

"I've got a two-pronged approach. One is a strategy for communicating with Roger and rescuing the ad campaign. Obviously, that is the most pressing concern for you and Creative Advertising. The second approach is a plan for the way you and I should collaborate going forward. I didn't realize until this past week that I need help from you and others to do my job effectively while I'm on the learning curve. I plan to be much more proactive in the future to get what I need to succeed—and not let you or the agency down."

Rhonda took a moment before replying. "There's no doubt the United Bank account is in crisis," she said. "If I had a dollar for every time we've had to rally to save a client I could retire. I need to get your update, but I'm confident we can save this one," Rhonda said.

Steve heaved a silent sigh of relief. Losing his job would have been bad enough, but the guilt from losing the account would have made it worse. He was reaching for the proposal to begin filling Rhonda in, but she wasn't finished.

"Frankly, Steve, I am more worried about you. I know how conscientious you are about your work, and the pride you take in doing good work. I don't want to lose you, but I feel you slipping away."

Steve could barely take it in. She was afraid of losing *him*? He blurted out what could have been the dumbest question he'd ever asked.

"You mean you aren't going to fire me?"

To his astonishment, Rhonda laughed. "I'm sorry," Rhonda said, trying to control her amusement. "I remember hearing a story—who knows if it's true, but it's a great story—about Tom Watson, the legendary leader of IBM. A young man sent to Watson's office was terrified because he'd been in charge of a project that had lost thousands of dollars—maybe millions. The number goes up every time I hear the story. Anyway, the young man went into this intimidating office and Watson said, 'Tell me what happened, what you learned, what went right, what went wrong.' So for an hour the young man spilled his guts, told Watson everything he thought was relevant. At the end of the meeting Watson thanked the young man and shook his hand. The young man sat there stunned and asked the same question you just asked me— 'You're not going to fire me?' You know what Watson said?"

Steve shook his head. "What?"

"Story has it that Watson bellowed, 'Fire you? I just spent thousands of dollars training you, why would I fire you?' " Rhonda laughed her hearty, full-throated laugh. "Steve, I'm in the same boat as Watson. I figure you've learned more in the last week than any MBA program could teach. I can't afford to fire you!"

Not one to trust good news immediately, Steve had one more question. "I heard rumors that you were going to replace me with Grant on the account."

Rhonda screwed up her face in a look Steve couldn't decipher. He waited for her to respond. Finally she said, "Remember the children's game of telephone, where one kid whispered a message in another's ear, and that kid passed it to the next kid, and by the time the message got back around it was a total distortion of the original message?"

"So what was the original message?" Steve asked.

"It wasn't a message; it was just an idea I was considering. Grant has real potential and wonderful people skills, but he lacks focus and attention to detail—the very qualities you have in spades. My thought was to have him become your junior account executive so you could teach him a wider variety of skills."

Steve felt like jumping for joy. "Well, if you're not firing me, and I'm not quitting, I guess we've got a lot of work to do. And I obviously have a lot to learn before I start mentoring Grant. Let's order lunch and I'll show you my plans." Steve signaled Tina, who was on the spot in a second.

As they ate, Steve showed the United Bank proposal to Rhonda, explaining why he thought the client rejected the budget, production plan, and creative approach. "I was a master budget and schedule-maker when I assisted you, but I didn't— I don't—know how to gather the right information and get buy-in from the client. Those were your responsibilities that I never learned to do."

Steve had decided to avoid using the D-laden language of the Needs Model. The model would guide his thoughts and comments, but he feared it would confuse things to speak a language Rhonda didn't know. But as he shared his insights he remembered how much easier it had been to communicate with Blair when they both spoke the language. So he pulled out the Needs Model and gave Rhonda a brief overview.

Rhonda was more than receptive. She asked for specific examples. Steve pulled out the sheet where he had prioritized his goals, diagnosed his development level on each, and determined the leadership style he needed. He explained to Rhonda that she wasn't the only one he would rely on for leadership.

"I've challenged the assumed constraints I had about my team and the client. I've also celebrated my points of power and come to realize there are many people and resources available to me. In other words, you're not the only one who can lead me."

Rhonda seemed relieved that the responsibility was not entirely hers. "So you're saying:

❋

A Leader Is
Anyone Who
Can Give You the
Support And Direction
You Need
To Achieve
Your Goal.

❋

"That's right!" Steve said brightly. "But, as my mentor, coach, boss, and right now, savior of the United Bank account, I need as much direction as I can get from you."

"Well, here it comes," Rhonda warned. "The reason this presentation failed is because you focused on what you were comfortable with and missed the point. You attempted to use the budget and production schedule to drive the strategy. It's got to be the other way around. Strategic approach first, then creative, then budgets and schedules. You went with what you knew, but in this case it took you in the wrong direction. That's why Peter and Alexa couldn't come up with anything creative. They were working in a vacuum."

"But I couldn't get the client to come up with or agree on a strategy," Steve groaned.

"Steve, I'm going to turn your Needs Model upside down on you here. Has United Bank ever mounted a full-blown ad campaign before? Have they ever worked with an ad agency, let alone our ad agency, before? Are Roger and his reps advertising experts?"

Steve looked at Rhonda, to the Needs Model, and back to Rhonda as the realization hit him. He had abandoned United Bank just as he'd felt Rhonda had abandoned him. They didn't have a clue how to give him a strategy.

"Talk about the blind leading the blind," Steve conceded. "They were Enthusiastic Beginners at D1 and now I'm sure they are Disillusioned Learners at D2 on the entire process. We need to give them High Direction and High Support to get buy-in for the strategy."

Steve pulled out his Palm Pilot. "Rhonda, I know that getting very specific with timelines and action steps isn't your favorite thing—you're a big-picture thinker—but it's what I need to make this work."

Rhonda smiled and pulled out *her* Palm Pilot. Together they made a plan for saving the client.

At Steve's signal, Tina slipped him the check and a questioning look. She motioned, *Thumbs-up or thumbs-down?* Steve replied with an under-the-table double thumbs-up. In a quiet voice he said, "Thanks for your graciousness, and keep the change." He gave her a wink and a generous overpayment of the bill.

9

One Minute Magic

Steve stood behind the stage, speaking softly to the audiovisual technician through his headset. He was again the coproducer of this year's advertising awards program. The master of ceremonies announced the next category: Best of Show for overall advertising campaign. As the five finalists were read, Steve peeked out at the audience. Rhonda and Grant were sitting in the third row with Roger from United Bank. Steve hoped they wouldn't be too disappointed.

The MC opened the envelope. "The winner is"— he paused—"Irma's Eatery!" A whoop went up from the crowd as the names of the creative team and ad agency were announced.

Steve watched Rhonda reach over and give Roger a consoling pat on the arm. *Just wait,* he thought.

The MC handed out the triangular-shaped crystal trophies and waited for the applause to wind down before making the next announcement. "This year the panel of judges added a new category—the Judges' Award for Best of Show among new advertisers. And that award goes to—United Bank!"

Steve watched Roger jump up from his seat and grab Grant by the shoulders. Steve laughed out loud at seeing the staid bank president so animated. Roger had turned out to be an ideal client. As the MC recognized Creative Advertising and the United Bank team: Peter for art direction, Alexa for copywriting, Maril for media buying, Jude for production, Grant as junior account executive, and Steve as account executive. The proud-mama look on Rhonda's face was priceless. Steve found himself happier for the others than for himself.

The nine months since Rhonda and Steve met at Irma's Eatery had been intense. It was only fitting that the restaurant chain should win the big award and that Creative Advertising should win the surprise award of the evening. Steve was grateful to Rhonda and his team, but also to his two best collaborators for success—Blair and Cayla. Blair had grown from girlfriend to wife and from beginning runner to fledgling marathoner, trusting the Needs Model to help her master long-distance running and their new marriage. Steve continued to be mentored by Cayla, though not as frequently as in the beginning. Steve felt a pang of sadness—there was no Cayla sighting this night. He had become used to his favorite magician popping up at the strangest yet most appropriate times.

Steve tied up loose ends backstage, thanked the MC for a job well done, and joined the small group of people still chatting in the lobby. They broke into applause as he walked in. There were bear hugs and pats on the back from coworkers, colleagues, friends, and of course, Blair. Suddenly Steve felt a tug at his arm. It was Rhonda.

Pulling him aside, she cupped her hand over his ear and whispered, "Meet me in my office first thing Monday morning." She winked and was off.

*   *   *

On Monday, Steve greeted Phyllis—who was now his secretary as well as Rhonda's. "The boss wants to see me. Any idea why?"

Smiling her Mona Lisa smile, Phyllis refused to divulge anything.

Hearing Steve's voice, Rhonda came out to usher him into her office. "Steve," she said as she shut the door, "I ran an idea past Roger, and he's in agreement pending your input. I want to pull you off United Bank and promote Grant to account executive."

Steve didn't respond, hoping there was more to the story. Rhonda took it as a sign to continue. "I want to promote you to head of the new business development department. If we land an account that is especially attractive to you, you have the option to take it on as an account executive. What do you think?"

Steve processed the news for a moment before saying, "The idea intrigues me. My concern is that I'd leave a position where I'm at the D4—High Achiever stage on most of my goals for a position where I'm at the D1—Enthusiastic Beginner stage on almost every goal. It's not only a new position for me, but for the agency."

"That's why we want you," Rhonda said emphatically. "The role needs someone who will shape it. Someone who will challenge the assumed constraint that 'it's never been done before.' Someone who will celebrate points of power to draw upon resources such as me and my partners who have been responsible for new business since we started the company. Someone who knows how to collaborate for success to get the direction and support needed to succeed in the role."

Steve was flattered—especially after Rhonda alluded to salary and benefit increases. Still—not motivated by money, power, or status and never one to make snap decisions, Steve told Rhonda he'd give her an answer the next day.

Steve would talk it over with Blair. But he also felt honor-bound to share the decision with his mentor.

❖ ❖ ❖

Steve parked directly in front of Cayla's Café. It had been weeks since he'd had a chance to visit her and sip a mocha. The familiar door chime announced his arrival. He checked out "their" table, and to his surprise, saw Cayla sitting with a jovial-looking fellow who seemed somehow vaguely familiar. When Cayla spotted Steve, she smiled and waved.

"Come here!" she called. "I have someone I'd like you to meet."

Steve walked over and extended his hand to the familiar stranger. "Hi, I'm Steve," he said.

The man gave Steve an earnest handshake. "Pleased to meet you, Steve. I'm—"

"The one-and-only One Minute Manager!" Cayla chimed in. "This is the guy who taught me everything I know about the magic of self leadership."

Steve's face lit up. "Wow! It's great to meet you," he said. "I can't tell you how much your teaching has changed my life for the better."

The One Minute Manager smiled humbly. "I feel as though I know you. Cayla has told me all about you. You should feel very proud."

Steve smiled. "When I tell her the latest good news, Cayla's the one who'll feel proud. I also need her advice about an offer my boss made me. But wait, I'm interrupting you. I'll be glad to come back later."

"Ha!" the One Minute Manager let out a hearty laugh. "How can you refuse him, Cayla? He used the 'I need' phrase."

Cayla laughed and signaled Steve to sit down. Steve told them about United Bank's win at the ad awards program and his pride for his team's success. Then he outlined his new job opportunity.

"Congratulations, Steve." Cayla turned to the One Minute Manager and said, "I guess it's time."

"Time for what?" Steve asked apprehensively.

"To let you go," Cayla responded.

Steve looked to her, then to the One Minute Manager, for an explanation.

"Steve," he said, "the beauty of developing a self leader is that it ultimately frees managers to focus their attention where it's most needed. Cayla's job was to teach you how to be a self leader. She accomplished her goal. It's time she turned her attention to others who need her."

"But I'm not at the High Achiever level on everything. I still need direction and support," Steve protested.

"You may not be at the High Achiever level on many of the goals and tasks required in your new job opportunity," the One Minute Manager said firmly, "but you've mastered the three tricks of self leadership:

❈

Self Leaders:

Challenge Assumed Constraints,
Celebrate Their Points of Power,
And Collaborate For Success.

❈

"Just continue to practice the tricks and you'll manage yourself to success. There are other would-be self leaders who need Cayla now," he said.

The café door burst open and a gaggle of children rushed in, heading straight for Cayla's Magic Corner.

"Uh-oh!" Cayla said as she jumped from her chair. "Show time!"

"Cayla," Steve said as he grabbed her elbow, "before you go, how can I thank you? How can I ever repay you for your help?"

"Just be yourself," Cayla responded.

Before Steve could say more, Cayla was in front of the eager children, perched on her stool, looking intently at each one of them as she gained their attention. In her rich voice she said, "My name is Cayla, and I am a magician."

When the applause subsided, Cayla glanced at Steve as she asked the spellbound children, "Do you believe in magic?"

Steve smiled. *What do you know—I **do** believe in magic,* he thought. At that moment, he felt a tap on his shoulder.

"Good on you!" the One Minute Manager whispered into his ear. "You'll make a fine magician."

"What do you mean?" Steve whispered back.

The One Minute Manager simply pointed to a forlorn-looking woman sitting alone at a table. With her faraway stare, she looked as Steve must have looked when he first met Cayla.

The One Minute Manager winked and rose from his seat, heading for the exit.

As he watched the One Minute Manager disappear through the door, Steve suddenly knew how he would thank Cayla. He wouldn't do it by repaying her directly. He would thank her by carrying on the legacy of the One Minute Manager. He would:

❋

*Teach Others
The Magic
Of Self Leadership*

❋

THE END

 *Appendix*

The Business Card Trick

Can you cut a hole from a business card large enough to stick your head through? This trick demonstrates the power of challenging assumed constraints. To master it, follow these four steps:

1. Take a business card and fold it in half lengthwise. Starting from the folded edge, cut a series of slits one-quarter inch apart to within about one-half inch of the opposite side.

2. Turn the card completely around so that the open edges are facing you. Between the slits, cut more slits going in the opposite direction, stopping about one-half inch from the opposite end of the card.

3. Slip the scissors into the fold starting after the first slit. Cut along the folded edge, stopping at the last slit, being careful to leave one-quarter inch of the fold intact at each end.

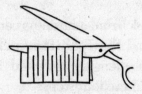

4. Carefully unfold the card, pulling the slits apart as wide as they will go, and slip the paper ring over your head.

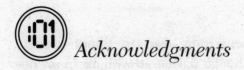 *Acknowledgments*

We would like to thank the people who have brought their own special magic to this book: **Martha Lawrence,** who helped shape not only this book but our hearts as well; **Maril Adrian,** who shepherded Situational Self Leadership and the EDGE to their success; **Linda Taylor,** who shared her expertise of learning and accelerated learning theory; **Linda Hulst, Patrice DeVeau Simpson,** and **Charlene Ables,** who took personal interest—not just professional interest—in improving the quality of this book; clients and colleagues who took time from their busy lives to provide feedback and support, especially **The Marmaxx Group** and **Nancy Maher; Jim Martin** of Dow Chemical; **Humberto Medina, Trevor Keighly, Victoria Cutler, Carla de Bose, Jason Arnold, Richard Andrews, Debra Talbert,** and **Mark Manning** of The Ken Blanchard Companies; all the good folks at the Skaneateles Country Club, who gave us feedback; and our brilliant editor at William Morrow, **Henry Ferris.**

Susan: I would like to personally thank: **Kenny Taylor,** who teaches wisdom through the martial arts and self leadership through application; **Peter Turner,** who taught me to take magic seriously; **Bill**

Brown, who opened my eyes to things unseen; **Aubrey Keen,** who has partnered with me in my on-going search for self-knowledge; **Kip Woodring,** for his support over many years, his motorcycling wisdom, and his classic parts-salesman song.

We all wish to thank our partners. Ken thanks his wife, **Margie,** who has been an inspiration and learn-ing partner for over forty years. Susan thanks **Drea Zigarmi,** her mentor and life partner, whose passion about leadership is exceeded only by his passion for good thinking; Laurence thanks **Laurie Ozanne Hawkins,** who has been part of the Blanchard journey all the way.

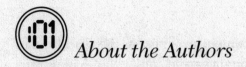 *About the Authors*

Few people have made a more positive and lasting impact on the day-to-day management of people and companies as **Ken Blanchard.** He is the author or coauthor of several bestselling books, including the blockbuster international bestseller *The One Minute Manager* and the giant business bestsellers *Leadership and the One Minute Manager, Raving Fans,* and *Gung Ho!* His books have combined sales of more than fifteen million copies in more than twenty-five languages. Ken is the chief spiritual officer of The Ken Blanchard Companies, a worldwide human resource development company. He is also cofounder of the Lead Like Jesus Ministries, a nonprofit organization dedicated to inspiring and equipping people to be servant leaders in the marketplace. Ken and his wife, Margie, live in San Diego and work with their son, Scott, daughter, Debbie, and Debbie's husband, Humberto Medina.

Susan Fowler has been a consulting partner with the Ken Blanchard Companies since 1990. With Ken Blanchard and Laurence Hawkins she created—and is the lead developer of—Situational Self Leadership, considered the best-of-class self leadership and personal empowerment program in the world today. During her twenty-five-year career she has written four popular guidebooks: *Overcoming Procrastination; Mentoring: How to Cultivate the Most Important Relationship of Your Career; The Team Leader's Idea-a-Day Guide: 250 Ways to Make Your Team More Effective Every Day of the Year* (with Drea Zigarmi); and *Empowerment: Achieving Peak Performance Through Self Leadership* (with Ken Blanchard).

Susan is one of the foremost experts on personal empowerment, having spoken in all fifty states in the U.S. and more than twenty foreign countries. In 2002 she received a lifetime achievement award for creative instructional design from Thiagi's North American Simulation and Games Association. She is cofounder of Leadership Legacies, LLC, a research group dedicated to the ongoing exploration of leadership practices and behaviors. She received her bachelor of science degree in business from the University of Colorado at Boulder and is currently an adjunct professor for the University of San Diego's Masters of Science in Executive Leadership degree program.

Laurence Hawkins is an internationally renowned management consultant and trainer and a dynamic motivational speaker. For the past twenty years he has worked with hundreds of organizations in the areas of leadership training, motivation, team building, and organizational development.

His international experience has won him consulting and training contracts in South America, the Far East, and several European countries, including Spain, Great Britain, Italy, Sweden, Holland, and Denmark. Domestically and internationally, he has earned the reputation of being a dedicated and well-versed professional who inspires positive results in a practical manner.

Laurie's client list includes a variety of industries and such corporate giants as Lockheed Martin, AT&T, Johnson & Johnson, and Bristol-Myers Squibb, as well as a number of schools, hospitals, restaurants, and start-ups.

With Ken Blanchard and Susan Fowler, he coauthored the Situational Self Leadership program, which focuses on empowerment and taking initiative when you're not in charge.

Laurie received his bachelor's degree in American history and literature from Williams College and his master's and doctorate degrees in leadership and organizational behavior from the University of Massachusetts, Amherst.

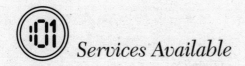 *Services Available*

Self Leadership and the One Minute Manager completes the trilogy that started with *Leadership and the One Minute Manager,* followed by *The One Minute Manager Builds High Performing Teams.* These three books describe the three leadership programs that have played a major role in building The Ken Blanchard Companies. Our company is committed to helping people and organizations lead at a higher level. With a mission to *unleash the power and potential of people and organizations for the greater good,* we are a global leader in workplace learning, productivity, and leadership effectiveness. We believe that people are the key to accomplishing strategic objectives. Our programs not only help people learn, but also ensure that they cross the bridge from learning to doing. We offer seminars and provide in-depth consulting in the areas of leadership, teamwork, customer service, performance management, and organizational synergy. To learn more, visit the Web site at www.kenblanchard .com or browse the eStore at *www.kenblanchard.com/ estore.*

UK

The Ken Blanchard Companies
Blanchard House
1 Graham Road
Wimbledon
London SW19 3SW

Tel: 44 (0)20 8540 5404
Fax: 44 (0)20 8540 5464
Email: uk@kenblanchard.com

Ireland

Blanchard Ireland
Brookfield House
Carysfort Avenue
Blackrock,
Dublin

Tel: 353 1 283 3500
Fax: 353 1 283 3592
Email: morgpier@iol.ie

Australia

Blanchard International Group
P.O. Box 374
Eastwood
NSW 2122

Tel: 61 2 9858 2822
Fax: 61 2 9858 2844
Email: pstapleton@ptd.com.au

New Zealand

The Blanchard International Group, NZ Ltd
P.O. Box 6549, Marion Square
Level 7, Presence House
57-59 Courteney Place
Wellington 6030

Tel: 644 385 9763
Fax: 644 385 9232
Email: Malcolm.Sutherland@blanchard.co.nz

USA

The Ken Blanchard Companies
125 State Place
Escondido
California 92029
USA

Tel: 1 760 839 8070
Fax: 1 760 489 8407
Email: International@kenblanchard.com